New Zealand

FODOR'S TRAVEL PUBLICATIONS

are compiled, researched, and edited by an international team of travel writers, field correspondents, and editors. The series, which now almost covers the globe, was founded by Eugene Fodor in 1936.

OFFICES
New York & London

Fodor's New Zealand

Editor: Kathleen McHugh
Area Editors: John Campbell, Marael Johnson, Graeme Kennedy
Maps: Pictograph
Drawings: Sandra Lang
Cover Photograph: Dallas and John Heaton/Miller Services

Cover Design: Vignelli Associates

SPECIAL SALES

Fodor's Travel Publications are available at special discounts for bulk purchases (100 copies or more) for sales promotions or premiums. Special editions, including personalized covers, excerpts of existing guides, and corporate imprints, can be created in large quantities for special needs. For more information, write to Special Marketing, Fodor's Travel Publications, Inc., 201 East 50th Street, New York, NY 10022. Enquiries from the United Kingdom should be sent to Merchandise Division, Random House UK Ltd, 30–32 Bedford Square, London WC1B 3SG.

Fodor's 89
New Zealand

Reprinted from *Fodor's Australia, New Zealand, The South Pacific 1989*

FODOR'S TRAVEL PUBLICATIONS, INC.
New York & London

ISBN 0–679–01681–3

MANUFACTURED IN THE UNITED STATES OF AMERICA
10 9 8 7 6 5 4 3 2 1

CONTENTS

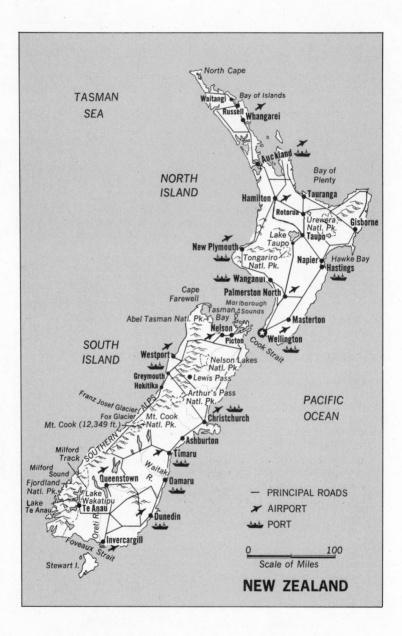

TASMAN
SEA

North Cape

Waitangi · Bay of Islands
Russell
Whangarei

NORTH
ISLAND

Auckland

Bay of
Plenty

Hamilton
Tauranga
Rotorua
Urewera
Natl. Pk.
Gisborne
Lake
Taupo
Taupo

New Plymouth
Tongariro
Natl. Pk.
Napier
Hawke Bay
Hastings

Wanganui
Palmerston North

Cape
Farewell
Marlborough
Sounds
Tasman
Bay
Masterton
Abel Tasman Natl. Pk.
Nelson
Picton
Wellington

SOUTH
ISLAND
Cook Strait

Westport
Nelson Lakes
Natl. Pk.

Greymouth · Lewis Pass
Hokitika

Arthur's Pass
Natl. Pk.
PACIFIC
OCEAN
Franz Josef Glacier
Fox Glacier
Mt. Cook
Natl. Pk.
Mt. Cook (12,349 ft.)
Christchurch

Ashburton

Milford
Track
Timaru

Milford
Sound
Waitaki
R.
Fjordland
Natl. Pk.
Queenstown
Oamaru

Lake
Te Anau
Lake
Wakatipu
Te Anau

— PRINCIPAL ROADS

Dunedin
✈ AIRPORT

Oreti R.
PORT

Invercargill

Foveaux Strait
0   100

Scale of Miles

Stewart I.

NEW ZEALAND

FOREWORD

New Zealand is a country of spectacular natural beauty: long, deserted beaches; glacial mountains; rich green forests and pastures. Here a wealth of activities await the active sporting enthusiast—hiking, skiing, fishing, rafting. Other visitors may enjoy the New Zealand scenery from the more relaxing vantage point of a boat or car, or prefer to spend days absorbed in the heritage of the Maori culture. Fine dining, first-class hotels, friendly people are all to be experienced in New Zealand.

Fodor's New Zealand is designed to help you plan your own trip to this country, based on your interests, your time, your budget—your idea of what this trip should be. Perhaps having read this guide you'll have some new ideas. We have, therefore, tried to put together a range of activities and within that range to offer selections that will be worthwhile, safe, and of good value. The descriptions we provide are designed to help you make your own intelligent choices from among our selections.

The first section of this book, Facts at Your Fingertips, consists of material designed to help you plan your trip, providing general information on how to get there, necessary travel documents, types of activities available, and local facts such as time zone, climate, and the like.

Next are introductory essays to help you with the background of the area: the people, the arts, some historical insights, and so on.

Following these essays comes the detailed description of the country by island. Each island is first broadly described; following is the Practical Information to help you explore each place: detailed descriptions, addresses, phone numbers, and so forth for accommodations, restaurants, tours, historical sites, museums, and more.

While every care has been taken to insure the accuracy of the information contained in this guide, the publishers cannot accept responsibility for any errors that may appear.

All prices quoted in this guide are based on those available to us at the time of writing. In a world of rapid change, however, the possibility of inaccurate or out-of-date information can never be totally eliminated. We trust, therefore, that you will take prices quoted as indicators only, and will double-check to be sure of the latest figures.

Similarly, be sure to check all opening times of museums and galleries. We have found that such times are liable to change without notice, and you could easily make a trip only to find a locked door.

When a hotel closes or a restaurant produces a disappointing meal, let us know, and we will investigate the establishment and the complaint. We are always ready to revise our entries for the following year's edition should the facts warrant it.

Send your letters to the editors of Fodor's Travel Publications, 201 E. 50th Street, New York, NY 10022. European readers may prefer to write to Fodor's Travel Publications, 30–32 Bedford Square, London, WC1B 3SG.

FACTS AT YOUR FINGERTIPS

FACTS AT YOUR FINGERTIPS

TOURIST INFORMATION. The *New Zealand Tourist and Publicity Department* was founded in 1901 to develop tourist amenities and stimulate tourism, and today it has Travel Commissioners in various parts of the world, from whom information on accommodations, transport, tours, and all aspects of travel may be obtained. *North America:* Suite 810, One Sansome Street, San Francisco, CA 94104, (415) 788–7404; Suite 1530, Tishman Building, 10960 Wilshire Boulevard, Los Angeles, CA 90024, (213) 477–8241; Suite 530, 630 Fifth Avenue, New York, NY 10111, (212) 586–0060.

Britain: New Zealand House, Haymarket, London, S.W. 1Y 4TQ, (01) 930–8422.

Australia: United Dominion's House, 115 Pitt Street, Sydney NSW 2000, (02) 233–6633; C.M.L. Building, 330 Collins Street, Melbourne, Victoria 3000, (03) 67–6621; Watkins Place, 288 Edward Street, Brisbane, Queensland 4000, (07) 221–3722; 16 St. George's Terrace, Perth, West Australia 6000, (09) 325–7347; 26 Flinders Street, Adelaide, South Australia 5000, (08) 231–0700.

Japan: Toho Twin Tower Building, 2F, 1–5–2 Yurakucho Chiyoda-ku, Tokyo 100, 508–9981.

Germany: New Zealand Government Tourist Office, 6000 Frankfurt A.M., Kaiserhofstrasse 7, Federal Republic of Germany, 0692 88189.

Canada: New Zealand Consulate-General, 701 West Georgia St., IBM Tower, Vancouver, B.C. V7Y 186, (604) 684–2117.

Singapore: 13 Nassim Rd., Singapore 1025, 235–9966.

Within New Zealand the department operates *NZTP Travel Offices* (previously known as Government Tourist Bureaus) in: Auckland, 99 Queen St., (09) 798–180; Rotorua, 67 Fenton St., (073) 85–179; Wellington, 27 Mercer St., (04) 739–269; Christchurch, 65 Cathedral Square, (03) 794–900; Dunedin, 131 Princes St., (024) 740–344; Queenstown, 49 Shotover St., (294) 282–32.

These offices not only provide information but also offer a complete travel service in advising on and reserving sightseeing and in planning itineraries and making reservations if required. Such a service is, of course, also provided by the many travel agents, but the New Zealand Travel Offices are widely used by New Zealanders themselves for domestic travel arrangements.

Maps, touring information, and accommodations guides are also available from Automobile Association offices. See "Hints to the Motorist," below.

PASSPORTS, VISAS, CUSTOMS. A passport valid for 3 months beyond intended stay is required, except for nationals of Australia and the Commonwealth countries who have permission to reside indefinitely in Australia and New Zealand, but passports are necessary for re-entry into Australia.

No visas required for tourists from U.S., Japan, New Caledonia, and Tahiti, or citizens of West Germany, Iceland, and Malta for stay of not more than three months; citizens of Belgium, Denmark, Finland, France, Liechtenstein, Luxembourg, Monaco, Netherlands, Norway, Sweden, and Switzerland for stay of not more than six months. Commonwealth citizens require only temporary entry authority, which may be granted on arrival; those not wholly of European origin must obtain authority to enter before departure. Sufficient funds for length of stay and onward ticket required.

Visa applications at nearest New Zealand embassy or consulate or at British consulates. Allow two weeks by mail.

There is no restriction on the amount of foreign currency that may be brought into or exported from New Zealand. No customs duty is payable on personal effects, or on a reasonable amount of photographic equipment. No duty on: 1 qt. of liquor; 1 qt. of wine; 200 cigarettes or 50 cigars.

1

CLIMATE. Subtropical in the North Island; temperate in the South Island. The north has no extremes of heat or cold, but winter can be somewhat cold in the south. The seasons are reversed from the northern hemisphere: summer from December through February; fall from March through May; winter from June through August; spring from September through November.

Average Temperature (°Fahrenheit) and Humidity

Auckland	Jan	Feb	Mar	Apr	May	June	July	Aug	Sept	Oct	Nov	Dec
Average max. day temperature	74°	75°	73°	68°	63°	59°	58°	59°	62°	64°	68°	71°
Days of rain	6	5	6	8	10	12	12	11	9	9	8	7
Humidity, percent	64	65	65	65	70	71	69	69	66	65	64	66
Christchurch												
Average max. day temperature	71°	71°	67°	63°	57°	52°	51°	54°	59°	63°	67°	69°
Days of rain	5	4	5	4	6	6	6	4	4	5	5	5
Humidity, percent	57	59	63	65	71	70	70	63	61	56	55	58

Although there are good ski fields in both the North and South islands, snowfalls are largely confined to the mountainous area. Christchurch and Dunedin are the only two cities likely to experience an occasional fall of snow, which is usually light and quickly disappears.

PACKING. Take light- or medium-weight clothing during the summer (December-April) and medium weight at other times. Include a sweater for possible use at nights during the spring and fall to offset occasional cool days or when sightseeing in the mountainous regions. Include a raincoat for occasional rainy days.

New Zealanders tend to dress casually and informally, but a jacket and tie are usually worn when dining at top hotels and restaurants.

Shorts for men and women and slacks for women are acceptable. In general, dress as you would at home.

Don't forget sunglasses, sun hat, and sunburn protective creams (or buy them here). New Zealand is renowned for the clarity of its light—meaning that sunburn can occur more quickly and imperceptibly here than in many other places.

WHAT WILL IT COST? By comparison with most other countries, New Zealand is not expensive. The biggest variation is in accommodations. Rates for a room at the very top city hotels can be from NZ$100 up, at a very good motel from NZ$70 to NZ$100. At good, clean, comfortable quality hotels, rates could drop to NZ$90, and at motels to NZ$60. There are also a number of small guest houses with common bathrooms and toilets, often providing breakfast, for around NZ$30 to NZ$40.

Other than a 10% goods-and-services tax (GST) on all saleable items and services, there are no national or city taxes on accommodations or meals. (The GST may be increased in late 1988 to 12.5%.) A $2 airport tax is payable on departure overseas but not for domestic traveling.

CURRENCY. The monetary unit is the New Zealand dollar. Following recent devaluation, it is worth approximately US67¢. An American virtually buys everything at half price. The rate varies as the New Zealand dollar is "floating." Paper money is in denominations of $1, $2, $5, $10, $50, and $100; coins in 1-cent, 2-cent, 5-cent, 10-cent, 20-cent, and 50-cent pieces.

American Express, Diners Club, Bankcard, MasterCard, and Visa traveler's checks and credit cards are universally negotiable.

Prices quoted are in New Zealand dollars, unless otherwise noted.

HOW TO GET THERE. The international airports at Auckland, Wellington, and Christchurch have direct services to Australia, but most international flights arrive at Auckland. *Air New Zealand,* the national carrier, serves most major gateways, among them Los Angeles, Vancouver, London, Tokyo, and Hong Kong. *United Airlines, Continental Airlines,* and *UTA French Airlines* have regular flights from North America. Other carriers with service to New Zealand include: *Canadian Airlines* from Vancouver; *Hawaiian Airlines* from Honolulu; *Qantas* from North America and Europe, via Australia; *British Airways* from London; *Japan Airlines* from Tokyo; *Singapore Airlines* from Singapore; *Cathay Pacific* from Hong Kong; and *Thai International* from Bangkok.

STOPOVERS. Air carriers have opened many Pacific doors with their new online stopover privileges. You must work with your travel agent, but to give you an idea of how this works investigate "circle" fares. Low season is always the best bargain dollarwise, and circle fares mean multi-destinations for you. Remember these are special fares; you cannot change carriers. Stopover or multi-destination examples: *Air New Zealand's* low-season fare of $1,295 from Los Angeles includes stopovers in Honolulu/Fiji/Auckland with return via Cook Islands and Tahiti/Los Angeles. For an extra $100 you can add Wellington and Christchurch to your itinerary and continue to Sydney or Brisbane with a return to Auckland, Cook Islands, and Tahiti/Los Angeles.

HOW TO GET AROUND. By air: *Air New Zealand* provides frequent service between major cities and main provincial centers; *Ansett New Zealand* has regular flights between Auckland, Wellington, and Christchurch. Scheduled flights to some of the outstanding scenic areas are operated by *Mount Cook Airlines* and *Ansett New Zealand.*

Air New Zealand Pass: 60-day passes valid for four or six legs begin at $280. *Ansett New Zealand Air Pass:* ranges from $400 to $720 for four to eight days. *Kiwi Air Pass:* allows 14 days of travel to:

Bay of Islands, Auckland, Rotorua, Christchurch, Mt. Cook, Queenstown, and the Southern Lakes. (Not valid for flightseeing, ski-plane, or charter operations.) Reservations are essential and must be made at the Mount Cook Airlines offices in New Zealand. Tickets must be issued against the pass only by Mount Cook in New Zealand, and only for each separate stage of the itinerary. Rates are for air travel only, all other charges at passenger's expense. Contact Mount Cook Line, Suite 1020, 9841 Airport Blvd., Los Angeles, CA 90045; (213) 684–2117. All air passes must be purchased prior to arrival in New Zealand.

By rail: The main towns and cities of both islands are connected by rail, and many of the routes are quite scenic. Wellington and Auckland have commuter train services. *New Zealand Railways* Travelpass allows unlimited rail travel throughout both islands. You can buy more than one pass if you want to travel, stay somewhere for a time, then travel again. Contact New Zealand Tourist Offices (see Tourist Information, above).

By bus: Scheduled coach service throughout the country. Rates run around NZ$16 to NZ$22 for a half-day trip; NZ$19 to $46 for a full day, depending on length of journey. Reservations required. Contact the Mount Cook Line or *Newmans Coachlines,* Box 3719, Auckland, or 10351 Santa Monica Blvd. #305, Los Angeles, CA 90025; (213) 552–0901. A *Kiwi Coach Pass* is available for reductions on bus fares.

By ferry: Ferries link North and South islands; travel is between Wellington and Picton and takes about 3½ hours. The service (52 miles across the Cook Strait) is operated by New Zealand Railways aboard three ferries for passengers, automobiles, and railway freight cars. Daily sailings from Wellington are at 10 A.M. and 4 P.M. daily, and 6:40 P.M. Monday through Saturday; with somewhat similar departures from Picton. Crossing takes 3 hours 20 minutes. Lounges, cocktail bars on board. Cabin berths available on some ships at extra charge. One-way passenger fare NZ$25. The voyage is scenic: the first 40 minutes are in Wellington Harbour, followed by a two-hour traverse of the lower end of the North Island thru Cook Strait, after which the ship enters the narrow gap of Tory Channel and steams for an hour down the sheltered deep-blue waters of Queen Charlotte Sound to Picton. In Wellington call 725–3990 or contact New Zealand Tourist Offices listed above under "Tourist Information."

HINTS TO THE MOTORIST. Except for the fact that traffic keeps to the left on the road and that automobiles are therefore right-hand drive, visitors should find no difficulty driving in New Zealand. All the main highways and secondary roads are well formed and sealed and well sign-posted, and state highways are numbered—a red shield being used for the main highways and a blue shield for secondary roads. Four-lane motorways are confined to approaches to main centers. Distances are given in kilometers.

The maximum speed limit is 100 kilometers per hour, but this is reduced to 50 kilometers in cities and more populous areas. A sign "L.S.Z." (Limited Speed Zone) means there is no speed limit set, but that the speed should be governed by road conditions and the traffic at the time.

School patrols control traffic at school crossings, and school buses should be passed with great care; you should stop if a bus is discharging children. A stop sign at an intersection means exactly what it says.

Giving way to other traffic is governed by what is known as the right-hand rule, which means that in general you always give way to traffic approaching from your right unless the other automobile is approaching you head-on and wants to turn across you or is approaching a give way sign (usually marked with double white lines on the road) on your right.

Most main highways have a broken white line at the center of the road, which means you can pass if the road is clear ahead. A double solid yellow line means don't pass, and a double yellow line with one solid and the other broken means that you can pass with care if the broken line is on your side.

Being a semi-mountainous country, New Zealand has few long, straight stretches of road. This makes for more interesting driving, but it also means that traveling times are often longer than might be expected from the distance to be covered.

Allowing for refreshment stops, gas replenishment, and occasional stops to admire the scenery, budget on an average of 50 to 60 kilometers per hour for comfortable driving.

Gas stations are scattered along the main routes, but make sure your tank is topped up before driving from Te Anau to Milford Sound and back. The return trip is only about 150 miles, but there is no habitation or gas station.

Watch out for sudden encounters with a herd of cows being driven home for milking or a flock of sheep being moved from one field to another. The farmer's dogs will usually clear a pathway for you.

New Zealand is tough on drinking and driving and has compulsory breathalyzer and blood tests.

The automobile association has branches at all the main centers and offers a comprehensive range of traveling brochures, maps, and accommodations guides. The main offices are at: Auckland, 33 Wyndham St. (774–660); Wellington, 344 Lambton Quay (851–745); Christchurch, 210 Hereford St. (791–280); Dunedin, 450 Moray Pl. (775–945).

RENTAL AUTOMOBILES

Several well-known rental firms operate in New Zealand. *Hertz, Avis, Budget,* and *Letz* have depots in the main cities and provincial centers and at airports. Rates vary very little and depend on the type of size of the automobile. Japanese cars tend to predominate.

A current domestic or international driver's license is required. Driver's licenses from the U.S., Australia, Canada, and the U.K. are valid. All firms must offer comprehensive automobile insurance coverage, which costs about $10 a day, and third party personal insurance is compulsory.

Average rental rates are $47 a day for a Honda Civic and $51 for a Toyota Corolla with an additional 16 cents per kilometer; $47 a day for an automatic Ford Telstar with 20 cents per kilometer. There are reductions for longer hire periods. A two-berth camper van costs from $110 to $120 a day, depending on the season.

TAXIS. Taxis in New Zealand do not cruise for hire and are obtained from a sign-posted taxi stand or by phone. All fares are based on metered charges so that it is not necessary to establish a fare when engaging a taxi. Tipping drivers is not necessary and is not usually done unless they have given special service.

ACCOMMODATIONS. Accommodations in New Zealand are equal to international standards in terms of amenities and creature comforts, but hotels are not as large or elaborate as is often the case in some other countries. The emphasis is on cleanliness and comfort rather than ostentation.

Similarly, rates are not as high and the category of "expensive" (a relative term) means they are top grade and expensive from a New Zealander's point of view but not necessarily to an overseas visitor. The highest rate for a standard room in a moderate hotel would be about NZ$110, although rates in a more elaborate hotel would be from NZ$130 up.

Motor inns are of modern design and have single or family suites with a high standard of appointment, on-site parking, usually a restaurant attached, and liquor service. The average room rate is about $90.

Motels have self-contained units. Some include fully equipped kitchens. Hotels and motels usually have tea- and coffee-making facilities. Rates range from NZ$65 to NZ$80 for a double room.

Motor camps offering community washing, cooking, and toilet facilities are available at the principal cities and resorts, but campers are required to provide their own tents and equipment. **Cabin accommodations** are available at some. Tent and caravan sites cost from $5 to $10 and cabins from $15 per person per night according to the standard and season.

For all accommodations early reservations are recommended during the peak demand period of Christmas, January, and Easter, when most New Zealanders go on holiday. With the increase in tourist arrivals advance reservations are advisable from October through April, particularly in some of the remote but outstanding scenic areas.

The *Tourist Hotel Corporation* has a chain of hotels at such areas as Waitangi, Auckland Airport, Rotorua, Waitomo Caves, Wairakei, Tokaanu, Tongariro National Park, Mount Cook, Queenstown, Te Anau, Wanaka, and Milford Sound, and has a reservations telephone number in Wellington (733–689), which can be dialed without long-distance charges from Auckland.

FARM HOLIDAYS. If you're traveling by self-drive car you shouldn't miss the opportunity of spending at least one night on a farm, where you'll be treated as one of the family, sharing meals with the hosts and, if you wish, taking part in daily farm activities. Several organizations can arrange such visits, and most farming families in the schemes are more interested in meeting people than in making money. Visitors can choose the type of farm in which they are interested—dairying, sheep, cattle, cropping, and high-country farming.

Some homes provide private bathroom facilities for guests, though in other homes you are expected to share with the family. In all cases hygiene standards are high, and facilities will be convenient to the guest room.

The daily cost per person usually covers dinner, bed, and breakfast, and the average price will average about $80, including meals.

Reservations are essential and can be made through a travel agent or with: *N.Z. Farm Holidays,* Private Bag, Parnell, Auckland (09–394–780); *Farm Home and Country Home Holidays,* Box 31–250, Auckland (09–492–171); *Town and Country Home Hosting,* Box 143, Cambridge (071–27–6511); *Rural Holidays New Zealand,* Box 2155, Christchurch (03–61–919); *Home Stay/Farm Stay,* Box 630, Rotorua (073–24–895); *N.Z. Home Hospitality,* Box 309, Nelson (054–84–727).

FOOD. New Zealand food has earned acclaim for its quality. Lamb, especially spring lamb from October to January, is probably the most popular dish, but other favorites are beef (roasted or as steaks), pork, and, in some restaurants, venison, which comes from deer farms.

The country's extended coastline yields good catches of fish; five delicious varieties are blue cod, snapper, John Dory, grouper, and orange roughly. Seasonal delicacies are oysters (Auckland rock oysters are small and sweet, and Steward Island oysters much larger and plumper and stronger in taste), crayfish, scallops, and whitebait (a type of small smelt).

Vegetables are fresh and good and in variety. Try kumara, a native sweet potato.

Good locally produced fruit is always available, especially during the summer months. Don't miss kiwi fruit, which originated in China but is now widely grown and exported. Another interesting fruit is the tamarillo, a pear-shaped red or orange fruit.

For dessert, New Zealand claims as its own the Pavlova cake, a special type of large meringue cake with lashings of whipped cream. And, of course, the traditional apple pie is everywhere.

Visitors often say that New Zealand milk shakes are especially enjoyable because of the quality and richness of the milk. There are milk bars everywhere.

New Zealand also has a good variety of domestic wines, some of which have won international awards.

The free brochure, "Taste New Zealand," listing restaurants specializing in New Zealand food and food events, is available from Travel Commissioners overseas and N.Z. Tourist Offices (*see* Tourist Information).

DINING OUT. All the main hotels have excellent restaurants of international class, but dining out can be fun. Most restaurants favored by New Zealanders are small and, particularly in Auckland, often in unprepossessing buildings where the interior has been renovated and redecorated into cozy intimate oases catering to 80 people or less.

Emphasis is on good food rather than surroundings and obsequious service. Not that service is lacking; it's just more casual, which is the New Zealand way of life. Waiters and waitresses are often university students earning extra money, and if they do not have the polish of professional waiters and waitresses, they are friendly and enjoy meeting and talking with patrons. Servility does not rate at all, but civility and friendliness do. You don't *have* to tip, but if you do it is appreciated, not as something routine and expected but as an expression of thanks for good service and attention.

Many of the restaurants are licensed to serve liquor; some are not, but diners can bring their own. Check with the restaurant when reserving a table, which is advisable, especially on weekends.

Prices vary, of course, but the difference between a moderate and expensive restaurant is not that great. An average price for two at a moderate restaurant for soup, appetizer, main course, dessert, and coffee would be around NZ$50 to NZ$60. Restaurant bills are not taxed.

There are plenty of restaurants offering cooked lunches, but try a New Zealand–style lunch: patronize one of the ubiquitous coffee shops or tea shops where you select from cabinets displaying meat pies and pieces of deep-fried fish, cold meat or chicken with a mixed green salad, sandwiches with a bewildering range of fillings, assorted small cakes and fruit salads, and tea, coffee, or soft drinks. An average filling lunch would cost from $5 to $7.

Or, if it's summer and you'd like to be like many office workers, buy a take-away lunch and eat it in one of the nearby parks or beaches.

Or you can have American fast-food at McDonalds or Kentucky Fried Chickens.

DRINKING LAWS. New Zealand's drinking laws may be confusing to a visitor. The government has set up a commission to rationalize the morass of rules and regulations, but it will be two or three years before this is completed.

Liquor at a bar or at tables may be purchased only at licensed hotels, which have public bars, lounge bars, and cocktail bars; some have entertainment. Individual bottles of spirits or beer can be purchased only from the "bottle store" of hotels, but minimum quantities of two gallons can be bought at lower rates from liquor wholesalers.

Hotel hours vary slightly, but are generally from 10 A.M. to 10 P.M. Monday to Saturday inclusive, but no liquor can be sold to the public on Sundays. However, if you are a guest in a hotel you can be served drinks after 10 P.M. for as long as the hotel keeper wants to keep the house bar open, and on Sundays. You can also be served drinks on Sunday if you are having a meal at a hotel.

Liquor, including beer, cannot be sold at supermarkets or other stores. On the other hand, New Zealand and imported wines can be sold as individual bottles from wine shops, which cannot sell spirits or beer.

The term *licensed restaurant* means it can serve you spirits or wine with your meal, and the term *BYO* means the restaurant cannot serve you liquor but you can bring your own bottle of wine. The minimum age for the consumption of liquor is 20.

TIME ZONE AND BUSINESS HOURS. New Zealand standard time is 12 hours ahead of Greenwich Mean Time; 17 hours ahead of New York; 20 hours ahead of San Francisco. In other words, 12 noon in New Zealand is 4 P.M. the previous day in San Francisco, 7 P.M. in New York, and 2 P.M. in Honolulu. New Zealand is also two hours ahead of Sydney, Australia. From the last Saturday in October to the first Sunday in March the clock is put forward one hour.

Shops and banks are open five days a week and closed on Saturday and Sunday, but some shops are open on Saturday until noon. Shops are usually open from 9 A.M. to 5:30 P.M. and until 9 P.M. on Fridays. If you are cooking your own meals it is wise to stock up for the weekend on Friday, although most supermarkets are open on Saturdays and small food shops with a basic range of goods (milk, canned food, butter, soap powder, tobacco, etc.) and known as "dairies" are open seven days a week.

FESTIVALS AND SPECIAL EVENTS. January: *Auckland Cup Galloping* race meeting; *National Lawn Bowling Tournament* (varies); *N.Z. International Grand Prix,* Auckland; *Wellington Cup Galloping* meeting; *National Yearling Sales* (bloodstock sale of about 450 selected yearlings, held concurrently with Wellington Race meeting); *Anniversary Day Yachting Regatta* (Auckland), reputed to be the largest one-day regatta in the world.

February: *Auckland Cup Harness* racing meeting; *Festival of the Pines* (New Plymouth), music, ballet and cultural arts in outdoor amphitheater; *International Vintage Car Rally* (varies).

March: *Golden Shears Sheep Shearing Championships* (Masterton), with leading shearers competing; *Ngaruawahia Annual Regatta* (Hamilton), the only Maori Canoe Regatta held; *Wellington Galloping* race meeting.

March/April: *Easter Show* (Auckland), a mixture of displays of home services, manufactured goods, and farm animals, horse riding events, carnival sideshows and outdoor attractions.

April: *Rugby* football and *winter sports* seasons (other than skiing) open; *Highland Games* (Hastings), an elaborate gathering of participants in traditional Scottish costume for competitions in bagpipe playing, Scottish dancing, and Scottish sport such as tossing the caber and shot putting; *Metropolitan Harness* racing meeting (Christchurch).

May: *Skiing season* opens (depending on snowfalls); *World Ploughing Championships* (Christchurch), a contest in which the winner, pulling a plow behind a tractor, plows the cleanest and straightest series of furrows over a given area of grassland.

June: *Great Northern Hurdles and Steeplechase* meeting (Auckland); *Agricultural Fieldays* (Hamilton), displays of equipment.

July: *Wellington Hurdles and Steeplechase* meeting.

August: *International Ski Championships* (varies); *Grand National Hurdles & Steeplechase* meeting (Christchurch).

September: *Cherry Blossom Festival* (Hastings and Alexandra), a parade of decorated floats to celebrate the full blossoming of cherry blossom trees.

October: *Hawke's Bay Agricultural Show* (Hastings); *Waikato Agricultural and Pastoral Show* (Hamilton). Commonly abbreviated to A & P Shows, these are farmers' shows where stock are paraded and judged for prizes. Produce, including home cooking, is displayed. There are usually horse-riding events and always carnival-type entertainment and sideshows. Much like a U.S. state fair. New Zealanders take their own vacations mid-December through April, and tourist attractions tend to be more crowded at these times.

November: *New Zealand Cup* race meeting and *Trotting Cup* race meeting (Christchurch); *Canterbury Agricultural and Pastoral Show* (Christchurch).

SIGHTSEEING. If you're interested in escorted tours, contact your travel agent. Operators of escorted tours include: *Brendan Tours,* 15137 Califa St., Van Nuys, CA 91411; *Club Pacific,* 790 27th Ave., San Francisco, CA 94121; *Four Winds,* 175 Fifth Ave, New York, NY 10010; *Globus Gateway,* 727 W. 7th St., Suite 1040, Los Angeles, CA 90014; *Hemphill/Harris,* 16000 Ventura Blvd., Suite 200, Encino, CA 91436; *Japan Travel Bureau,* 45 Rockefeller Plaza, New York, NY 10111; *Maupintour,* 1515 St. Andrews Dr., Lawrence, KS 66046; *Dateline Tours,* Box 1755, Newport Beach, CA 92663.

Independent tours are run by: *Islands in the Sun,* 760 W. 16th St., Suite L, Costa Mesa, CA 92627; *Expanding Horizons,* 17581 Irvine Blvd., Suite 115, Tustin, CA 92680; *Jetset Tours,* 8383 Wilshire Blvd., Suite 450, Beverly Hills, CA 90211; *Network Travel Planners,* 1414 Second St., Suite 103, Santa Monica, CA 90401; *Newmans Tours,* 10351 Santa Monica Blvd,. Suite 305, Los Angeles, CA 90025; *Silver Fern Holidays,* Park Center One, 33400 8th Avenue South, Suite 232, Federal Way, WA 98003; *ATS/tourPacific,* 1101 E. Broadway, Suite 201, Glendale, CA 91205.

Because trips to the main cities alone will not do justice to the variety of attractions this country has to offer, listed here are some sample itineraries to help you get the most out of your trip. *North Island* (4 days): Day 1, Arrive Auckland; day 2, Auckland to Waitomo Caves to Rotorua; day 3, at Rotorua; day 4, Rotorua to Auckland. *South Island* (5 days): Day 1, arrive Christchurch; Day 2, Christchurch to Queenstown by air; day 3, at Queenstown; day 4, Queenstown to Mount Cook to Christchurch; day 5, depart Christchurch. *Both Islands* (10 days): Day 1: Arrive Christchurch; day 2, Christchurch to Lake Te Anau by air; day 3, day trip to Milford Sound by road; day 4, Lake Te Anau to Queenstown by air; day 6, at Queenstown; day 7, Queenstown to Mount Cook by air; day 7, Mount Cook to Rotorua by air; day 8, at Rotorua; day 9, Rotorua to Waitomo Caves to Auckland by road; day 10, depart Auckland. *Both Islands* (17 days): Day 1, Arrive Auckland; day 2, at Auckland; day 3, Auckland to Paihia (Bay of Islands); day 4, at Paihia (catamaran or launch cruise or day trip to Cape Reinga); day 5, Paihia to Auckland; day 6, Auckland to Waitomo Caves to Rotorua; days 7 and 8, at Rotorua; day 9, Rotorua to Christchurch by air; day 10, Christchurch to Lake Te Anau by air; day 11, day trip to Milford Sound; day 12, Lake Te Anau to Queenstown; days 13 and 14, at Queenstown; day 15, Queenstown to Mount Cook by air; day 16, Mount Cook to Christchurch by air; day 17, depart Christchurch or fly to Auckland for departure.

SPORTS. Because of its temperate climate and the abundance of its mountains, rivers, lakes, and the surrounding sea, New Zealand has a wide range of outdoor activities within a relatively compact area. The easiest way to enjoy them is to check with the New Zealand Tourist Offices (see Tourist Information, above), both locally and before your trip.

Sports most favored by overseas visitors because of their excellence are *trout fishing, salmon fishing,* and *big game fishing* and *hunting* (see Fishing and Hunting, below).

Backpacking: There are guided hiking trips in several parts of the country, but the most popular are the three- or four-day alpine "walks" over the Milford Track in Fiordland, walks through the Routeburn and Hollyford Valleys from Queenstown, and the Wanganui River Walk. Contact Routeburn Walk, Ltd., Box 271, Queenstown (phone 100). For the Hollyford Valley Walk: Fiordland National Park, Box 29, Te Anau.

For the Milford Track hike, contact Tourist Hotel Corp. of New Zealand, Box 2840, Wellington. Departures from Te Anau on Mondays, Wednesdays, Fridays with extra parties scheduled as required. Trek is sold as a five-day/four-night package ending at Milford Sound. Prices: Adults NZ$605. In the U.S., contact Southern Pacific Hotel Corporation, 1901 Avenue of the Stars, Suite 880, Los Angeles, CA 90067; (213) 557–2292.

Dane's Back Country Experiences, Ltd., Box 230, Queenstown, NZ (phone 1144), are backcountry specialists in whitewater rafting, hiking, fishing, airplane tours in the back country. Tours from three hours to five days.

Information about the national park system, walks, and scenic reserves can be obtained from tourist information offices or Dept. of Lands and Survey, Private Bag, Wellington; (04) 735–022.

Boating: Mainly in Auckland and the Bay of Islands, yachts may be chartered fully equipped with or without crews; only food and bedding are required.

Fiordland Cruises Ltd., Manapouri, operate three-day cruises in Doubtful Sound in Fiordland. Charges include transport, accommodations and meals.

Jet boat trips are operated on many rivers, ranging from one hour to a full day. Inquire locally.

Golf: Even small towns have golf courses, at which visitors are always welcome. Green fees range from about $5 to $10 per game. Golf is very popular and played year-round. Equipment can usually be rented.

Mountaineering: Probably no country can offer such a wide scope and variety of mountaineering as the Southern Alps, where Sir Edmund Hillary, the first to climb Mount Everest, did much of his early training. Mount Cook and Westland, from the nature of their country, attract more overseas climbers than other places.

River Rafting: Heavy-duty inflatable rubber rafts similar to those used on the Colorado River are used for journeys down rivers and through countryside not normally seen. Trips vary from three hours to 12 days. See also Backpacking.

Snorkeling and Scuba Diving: While good diving is available out of most cities and towns, the Poor Knights, off the coast of Tutukaka in Northland, offers the most spectacular diving.

Skiing: New Zealand has fine ski fields, close to accommodations centers, and with the complete absence of tree hazards. The main season in the North Island is from about mid-July to the end of October and in the South Island from early July to the end of September. The main ski fields are at *Mount Ruapehu* in the North Island and at *Coronet Peak,* and the *Remarkables,* Queenstown, and *Mount Hutt,* near Christchurch.

Alpine Guides (Mount Cook) Ltd., Box 20, Mount Cook, or New Zealand Government Tourist Bureau, Alcoa Bldg., Maritime Plaza, San Francisco, CA 94111, provides information on helisking, glacier skiing, Nordic skiing, and Alpine skitouring. Guided climbing, mountaineering courses and raft trips are available in summer.

Surfing: New Zealand's extremely long coastline offers surfers a wide variety of reef point, river bar and beach breaks. The best surfing is in Northland, the west coast of the North Island, Bay of Plenty, Gisborne, Wellington, and the east coast of the South Island.

Spectator Sports There are virtually no professional sports in New Zealand, and organizations stick zealously to their amateur status. The climate allows almost all outdoor sports to be played throughout the year. Just about any sport you can think of (except baseball, the substitute being softball, and ice hockey) has its followers. Most popular in summer are **cricket, tennis, swimming, yachting,** and **sailing.** Field sports are played in public parks, with no admission charges. In winter the passion is **Rugby football, soccer football,** and **hockey**—again in free public parks except for the main Rugby match, for which there is an admission charge of $3 or so. Another passion is **horse racing** (gallops and harness racing) and there are race meetings somewhere every Saturday. The best way to find out what's happening where you are is to check the local newspapers. Admission charges in race courses vary but are very reasonable.

Fishing and Hunting. *Deep-sea fishing* is one of New Zealand's most outstanding sports and fishing facilities are well developed. Boats, complete with all equipment, may be chartered at five major ports, all on North Island within 200 miles of Auckland.

Trout fishing is excellent in New Zealand's numerous rivers and lakes, which are abundant with rainbow and brown trout. Season varies somewhat in different areas, but all areas are open from Oct.-Apr., and Lakes Rotorua and Taupo have open season all year. A special trout-fishing license for overseas visitors valid for one month is available at $12 from any NZTP office. Guides: NZ$18–$NZ24/hr.

Hunting. Experienced, registered guides providing all camping, hunting and transportation equipment can be obtained by writing to the Fishing and Hunting Officer, Tourist and Publicity Dept., Private Bag, Rotorua. Guides (costing around NZ$350 per day, plus food and equipment) will usually arrange for entry permits to National Parks or private land. Duck, Canadian geese, swan, pheasant and quail have a three-week to two-month season beginning the first Saturday in May. See also the essay on Fishing and Hunting.

BEACHES. No place is more than 70 kilometers in a direct line from the sea, which means there are accessible beaches from one end of New Zealand to the other. The list of swimming beaches would be endless. No beach can be privately owned, and all can therefore be used by the public. The main cities and provincial centers have their favorite beaches for swimming and picnics and most are safe for bathing—some have lifeguard patrols.

Apart from the many beaches just north of the city, Auckland is notable for half a dozen popular beaches starting a couple of kilometers from the city center (Mission Bay, Kohimarama, St. Heliers), and similarly in Wellington there is Oriental Bay just three kilometers from the city. All are faced by expensive homes and apartment blocks.

SHOPPING. The best buys for the visitor are greenstone jewelry and sheepskin. Greenstone is a type of jade, deep or pale green in color. For centuries, the Maori made weapons and ornaments from it, and it is now used for attractive rings and brooches. Other, less expensive ornaments are fashioned from the irridescent blue-green shell of the *paua,* a large shellfish similar to the abalone. New Zealand sheepskins make wonderful floor mats, jackets, soft toys, and automobile seat covers, which keep the seat cool in summer and warm in winter.

Many imported products are sold duty-free to visitors throughout the country.

GAMBLING. Gambling is illegal. There are no casinos and no poker machines. The exception is that bets on horse racing may be placed on a totalisator (pari-mutuel system) at a racecourse or at one of the many Totalisator Agency Board's offices (the T.A.B.) in a city or town.

Every Saturday there is a national LOTTO drawing ($2 per entry) with substantial prizes. The national lottery ($3, $10, or $20, depending on the prize) is drawn at irregular intervals.

HINTS TO HANDICAPPED TRAVELERS. Within recent years considerable attention has been given to catering to the handicapped traveler in New Zealand, and the main hotels, motels, department stores, and public toilets have special facilities. Parking areas and buildings have spaces marked and reserved.

POSTAGE. To North America, letters and postcards cost $1.05 cents for the first 10 grams; aerograms 80 cents. Domestic postage is 40 cents for a surface letter and 55 cents for airmail.

ELECTRICITY. The current in New Zealand is different from that in the United States—220–240 volts, A.C., 50 cycles—and the wall sockets require a three-prong plug (the two top prongs are set at an angle, so the set of adapter plugs you have may not work here). All the larger hotels and many of the motels have electric shaver sockets in the bathroom designed to accept two-prong plugs and adapted to 110 volts. Bring an adapter if you need one; they are hard to find here.

TELEPHONES. To call New Zealand, you'll need to first dial the country code (64) then the area code for the particular city. When calling within New Zealand city to city dial zero before the city's code. Auckland is 9; Wellington, 4; Christchurch, 3. Other codes and costs are listed in the front of directories.

The telephone service is controlled by Telecom, a government-financed corporation, and telephones are rented at a flat fee. There is no charge for local calls except from pay phones (20 cents). A station-to-station call to North America costs $9.60 for three minutes, $2.75 for each added minute.

If you want to know the cost of a call, dial the tolls operator and ask for a price required call—shortly after the call is completed the operator will phone and advise you. Hotels and motels require that long-distance calls be placed through the switchboard operator.

A ringing tone is "Burr-Burr-Pause-Burr-Burr"; a busy tone is "Buzz-Pause-Buzz"; an unobtainable number is "Pip-Pip-Pip-Pause-Pip-Pip-Pip" (call the operator for assistance).

Emergency numbers (police, ambulance, fire, etc.) are listed in the front of directories, as are doctors and hospitals.

NEW ZEALAND

Land of the Long White Cloud

by
JOHN P. CAMPBELL

*A New Zealander, the author has traveled to every part of his country
through his work with the New Zealand Tourist and Publicity Department.
Currently focusing on travel writing, he contributes to a number of publications, including* Travel Digest.

To think of the South Pacific is to conjure up visions of tropical isles, warm
sandy beaches, waving palms, exotic forests, colorful Polynesians and lilting music. As a South Pacific country New Zealand has all these; yet it
also contradicts the popular image. Its scenery rivals the best of other parts
of the world, but it also has fine modern cities and is a major exporter
of food and manufactured products.

The atlas shows New Zealand as a slender, slanted outline close to the
bottom of the world. Astride a line midway between the equator and the
south pole, it appears small and isolated in the vast Pacific Ocean. In
shape, it resembles California; in size it exceeds Britain and equals the area
of Colorado. On the map, New Zealand seems to be dwarfed by the neigh-
boring continent of Australia; but Australia lies 1,200 miles to the west,
and it is a source of pained but resigned irritation to New Zealanders that
the two are often linked by the misleading term "Australasia". Naturally,
there is some affinity between the two peoples, but Australia and New Zealand are quite distinct, each having an individual character and landscape.

11

New Zealand comprises three main islands: the North Island (44,197 square miles); the South Island (58,170 square miles); and Stewart Island (676 square miles). From north to south the country is about 1,000 miles long, and no point is more than 70 miles from the sea. Two-thirds is mountainous; a region of swift-flowing rivers, deep alpine lakes and dense subtropical forest—known locally as "bush."

New Zealand has the best of climatic worlds. The climate ranges from subtropical in the north to temperate in the south. There are no extremes of heat or cold, and snow is usually confined to the mountains and high country. Rainfall levels vary, but since rainy days are evenly distributed throughout the year, there is no unduly wet season to be avoided.

Topsy-Turvy Topography

To those living in the northern hemisphere New Zealand is an upside-down country. The north is warmer than the south and the seasons are reversed: summer is from December to March, fall from April to May, winter from June to August, and spring from September to November. Even the visitor's sense of time needs adjustment. New Zealand has a universal time zone, set 12 hours ahead of Greenwich Mean Time; which puts it ahead of most other places too: noon in New Zealand is 7 P.M. the previous day in New York, for instance. In the summer period, the difference is increased by one hour by New Zealand daylight-saving time, which extends from the last Sunday in October to the first Sunday in the following March.

For thousands of years, after its last land bridges sank beneath the Pacific, New Zealand remained isolated. Evolution went its curious way, undisturbed by man or beast except for sea-blown birds from other lands. Safe from predators, some birds became lazy and abandoned flight. Gradually their wings atrophied to small stumps and they walked the earth for their food. Best known is the kiwi (pronounced *kee-wee,* and named for its cry), which has become, although unofficially, New Zealand's national emblem. New Zealanders are sometimes referred to, and refer to themselves, as Kiwis. About the size of a young turkey and rounded in shape, the kiwi has strong legs and an unusually long bill with two nostrils close to the tip, which it pokes about in the undergrowth in search of grubs. Being nocturnal, it is seldom seen in the wild, but there are several places where it can be viewed in specially constructed houses.

An emu-like bird ten feet in height, the *moa,* once grazed in New Zealand. A main source of Maori food, and materials for clothing, it was hunted to extinction. The tuatara lizard, about 18 inches long and with a third vestigial eye, is a living fossil. It evolved before the giant dinosaurs roamed the earth, lives a hundred years or more, and still exists as a protected species on certain offshore islands.

Finding the Forgotten

About 75 percent of New Zealand's native flora is unique, and includes some of the world's oldest plant forms.

This was the virginal land first sighted by the adventurous Polynesian voyagers some 600 years ago. They called New Zealand by a more colorful name—*Aotearoa* ("Land of the Long White Cloud"). To them, near death from thirst and starvation in their sea-battered canoes on a migratory voyage across hundreds of miles of ocean, the land first appeared as a long, low white cloud on the horizon. To Abel Tasman, the first European to sight New Zealand, it appeared as "a great land uplifted high."

Both descriptions are apt. As you approach by air, New Zealand often does appear as a long low cloud joining the sky and the sea, especially when you are flying from Australia to Christchurch and the long line of the Southern Alps rises to meet you.

New Zealand was unknown to Europeans until 1642 when Abel Tasman, the Dutch navigator, sighted it when seeking a southern continent. He had trouble with the Maoris, however, and sailed away after drawing a wavy line as a crude chart. He gave the land the name of *Nieuw Zeeland.* No one was interested until 1769, when Captain Cook and a Frenchman, De Surville, rediscovered it almost simultaneously; though neither was aware of the other's presence on the opposite side of the islands. It was Cook who circumnavigated New Zealand and found that Tasman's wavy line was actually a group of islands. In general, his chart is amazingly accurate.

From 1790 onward adventurous Europeans arrived to take lumber, flax, whales and seals, and lonely settlements grew up in Northland and on the West Coast of the South Island. They were wild, lawless and isolated. The main European settlement and headquarters for the whaling fleets was Russell (then known as *Kororareka*) in the Bay of Islands. It became known as "the hellhole of the Pacific."

The newcomers traded muskets with the Maoris, and the traditional inter-tribal wars became bloodbaths. But the newly-introduced European diseases took a heavier toll. Thousands of Maoris, having no immunity, died from epidemics of normally minor ailments, such as influenza and measles.

Arrival of "Law and Order"

Pressure was growing on Britain to make New Zealand a colony. Finally, the British government acted by sending Captain William Hobson as governor. On February 6, 1840, a week after his arrival, he officiated at the signing of the Treaty of Waitangi, by which the Maoris ceded sovereignty to the British Crown in return for the protection of law and order and the rights of ownership of their traditional lands and fisheries for all time.

This event is regarded as the beginning of modern New Zealand history, and the date is still observed as New Zealand's National Day.

Then features of American history began to repeat themselves. Disputes over land developed between the settlers and the Maoris, culminating in the "Land Wars" of 1860. They flared up spasmodically for years, and the last sparks were not extinguished until 1872. The settlers cleared the land and turned to sheep farming, but the invention in 1882 of refrigeration enabled the export of meat, butter, and cheese.

New Zealand's success in agriculture is due to its ability to grow superb grass and clovers, an equable climate, land management, and regular applications of fertilizer from the air (known as topdressing).

Agricultural exports provide the major source of the country's income. It has become the biggest exporter of sheep meat and dairy products in the world and the second largest exporter of wool. These three agricultural commodities account for 75 percent of the country's total exports, and a wide and expanding range of annual crops is also grown.

New Zealand is ideally suited to sheep farming. High-country farms concentrate on wool, while the more fertile lowlands (carrying up to 5 sheep per acre and sometimes even more) raise lamb and mutton. With over 55 million sheep, it is not surprising that New Zealand is the third largest producer and second largest exporter of wool in the world. It is also the world's largest lamb and mutton exporter, contributing 65 percent of the market, and rears 6.5-million beef cattle.

Because of the equable climate, dairy stock do not have to be housed in winter, and grass grows the year round. There are some 2,080,000 cows in milk in New Zealand. Butter and cheese are the main dairy exports, followed by casein and skim milk powder.

Most grain crops are grown for local consumption, a wide range of fruit is grown for export, and tobacco is grown and blended with imported leaf for the local market.

New Zealand also exports a wide range of manufactured articles to many parts of the world. About a quarter of the labor force is involved in manufacture, though most of the factories are small by overseas standards.

The biggest growths have been in light engineering, electronics, textile and leather goods, rubber goods, plastics, building materials, pottery and glassware, and furniture. One of the largest developments has been in carpets.

Large exports of pulp, newsprint, wood chips, and lumber come from one of the world's largest manmade forests, the Kaingaroa Forest of more than 364,000 acres of *radiata* pine, which mature in about 25 years (much faster than in their native American habitat).

Influence of the Military

Though far from Europe, New Zealand has not escaped its conflicts. In World War I New Zealand fought beside Britain, and World War II cost another heavy contribution in manpower and resources. Its land forces fought in Greece, Crete, North Africa, Italy, and the Pacific, more than 140,000 served overseas.

New Zealand became vulnerable as the Japanese began moving across the Pacific, but it did not recall its troops from the Middle East. Instead, it became a base for American forces. The Second Marine Division was based in Wellington, and it was from there that they embarked for what was to become the bloodbath of Guadalcanal. Many New Zealanders whose sons were fighting overseas took Americans into their homes and adopted them as their own, and when news of the grim casualties came back an air of grief enveloped the city. Many of the wounded returned to Wellington for recuperation, and some returned after the war, married New Zealand women, and settled.

Although established as a British colony, New Zealand quickly achieved self-government and has long been a fully independent nation, but remains a member of the British Commonwealth by choice. The head of state is Queen Elizabeth II, who is represented by a resident governor-general, appointed for a term of five years. The present governor-general, Sir Paul Reeves, appointed in 1985, is a Maori.

The New Zealand Parliament has a single chamber, the House of Representatives, with 92 members, among whom are four Maori members elected directly by Maori voters. The head of government is the prime minister, who is always the leader of the successful political party.

From the 1880s, New Zealand has often led the way in social welfare.

In 1984, the New Zealand Labor party came into power, pledging to make the nation a nuclear-free zone. This has led to a certain amount of tension between New Zealand and U.S. governments, since American warships are now banned from New Zealand waters.

Seeing the Best of New Zealand

It is easy to be misled by looking at New Zealand on an atlas. It appears smaller than it really is, especially when compared with its much larger neighbor Australia. But don't allow its size to persuade you that it can be seen in three or four days by taking excursions from the main cities. Its varied attractions are scattered throughout the thousand-mile length of the two islands and are often remote from major cities.

Visitors will miss a great deal if they do not allow enough time to see the best of both the North and South islands. It is possible to glimpse some of the highlights in a week, but having invested in the cost of reaching New Zealand the wise traveler will allocate at least ten days or two weeks, or perhaps even longer.

Climatically and scenically, the islands are like two entirely different countries. The only satisfactory way to enjoy these attractions is to travel progressively from place to place.

New Zealand's charms lie in the countryside, mountains and fiords rather than in the cities. In terms of European settlement, New Zealand is less than a century and a half old; so there are no ancient sights.

Certainly, at least one day should be spent in the major cities, each of which has its own individuality and charm, but most of the time should be devoted to the scenic areas.

Driving for Fun

The main cities are linked by road, air and rail, but many of the most beautiful regions are in the mountain fastnesses and can be reached only by road or air. Because of the varied countryside, road travel is exciting. There are no long monotonous distances to be covered. Because of the hilly to mountainous terrain the roads weave through an ever-changing landscape, bordered by lush green pastures dotted with sheep and cattle, or clothed in native forest.

All the main roads and most of the secondary roads are paved, well maintained, and signposted, with route numbers. New Zealand has changed to the metric system, and all road signs are now in kilometers. To convert kilometers to miles, divide by 8 and multiply by 5; e.g., 100 km per hour (the legal speed limit) equals 60 mph.

Getting around Fairly Easy

New Zealand has an efficient network of air, road, rail, and sea transport. The major domestic air carriers are the government-financed Air New Zealand, which uses Boeing 737 jets and F27 Fokker Friendship turbo-jet aircraft and services the main cities and provincial centers, and Ansett New Zealand, which uses Boeing 737s on its services between Auckland, Wellington, and Christchurch. Servicing the prime scenic resorts such as Rotorua, Mount Cook, and Queenstown are Mount Cook Airlines and Ansett New Zealand. Mount Cook Airlines also continues to Te Anau in Fiordland. Modern motor coaches are used on coach tours and scheduled services, and the New Zealand Railways, government owned, link the main and subsidiary centers. Group tours are operated by several companies. Rental cars are available at all the main centers, but the visitor should note that traffic travels on the left of the road. Motor caravans and campervans may be rented at the main centers.

The New Zealanders

A survey of visitors' impressions carried out by the Pacific Area Travel Association showed that memories of "a warm, friendly people" did much to account for New Zealand's popularity with travelers in the South Pacific. Friendliness is undoubtedly one of its greatest charms. New Zealanders are fiercely proud of their country, and they enjoy sharing its delights with others. To them, a visitor is a guest—not just another tourist. The growth of tourism has not affected the New Zealander's spontaneous willingness to go out of her or his way to welcome and assist the visitor. Their good nature has enabled the people to become a distinctive, unique nation.

The early settlers, and those who followed them, left Britain to escape from overcrowded slums, the limitations imposed by class barriers, and the lack of economic opportunity. These motives have formed the New Zealand character and an egalitarian society. Few are very rich and none are really poor. There are no slums or tenements, and by overseas standards, unemployment is relatively low.

The Unimportance of Position

An egalitarian attitude is universal. New Zealanders do not take kindly to servility. New Zealanders cannot abide being addressed by their surnames only; to them, this would imply inferiority. Honorifics (Mr., Mrs., etc.) are always used until first-name terms are reached—which happens quickly, if not immediately. They value and respect people for themselves, not social status or wealth, which leave them unimpressed.

The Maori People

No one really knows where the Maori (pronounced *"Mau-ree,"* not *"May-ori"*) originally came from. Tradition has it that they sailed to New Zealand in a migratory voyage from a land they called Hawaiki, which was not Hawaii but is thought to have been the Society Islands near Tahiti. It is generally believed that the islands of the Pacific were inhabited by people from Asia, although one theory is that the first settlers came from South America. All three propositions are matters of scholarly discussion and debate.

One thing is sure—the Polynesians were among the greatest long-distance sailors in the world. Legend relates that the first Polynesian voyager to sight New Zealand was Kupe about A.D. 950, who returned to Hawaiki and gave sailing instructions which were later followed by the migrating canoes. It is said that the next to come was Toi, in about 1150.

One of the reasons for our lack of positive knowledge is that the Maori had no written language. History was passed down by word of mouth, usually in the form of chants (*waiata*). There was room, therefore, for imaginative embellishment.

Maori tradition has it that the great migration from eastern Polynesia took place about 1350 in seven canoes. No one knows why the migration took place, but it may well have been due to overpopulation and a shortage of food. If the great migration theory is believed, however, it is clear that the Maori knew of the existence of New Zealand and navigated to it in a voyage covering hundreds of miles—a remarkable achievement.

It now seems likely, however, that the canoes arrived over a period of years, even centuries, rather than all at once in a "Great Fleet." It's thought that the original settlers probably arrived by the eighth century.

The earliest arrivals are known as *moa* hunters. They had an abundance of food from the *moa* (a huge bird), other flightless birds, and fish from the sea. Their villages were unfortified, they seem to have had no weapons. Later, conflict did develop.

The Maori brought with them the *kumara,* a variety of sweet potato, the dog, and the rat. These were the first mammals to live in New Zealand. The Maori had an abundance of fish and birds and established agriculture.

From these beginnings emerged a distinctive Maori culture and well-ordered tribal society, led by hereditary chiefs and a powerful priesthood.

The Maori lived in small villages retreating to hilltop fortifications (*pa*) during times of war. They built sleeping and eating houses and a main meeting house, all focused on a main courtyard, the *marae*. The *marae* was an important part of the village. It was here, in front of the meeting house (*whare runanga*), that matters of importance were debated and decided and that visitors were received.

Lore of the Tribes

The *marae* retains that importance and function today. Though they now live in European-style homes, any large settlement of Maoris will have a meeting house and a *marae* on which any important visitors will be received, and an ancient and impressive greeting ritual is still followed.

Intensely proud, the Maroi also practiced *mana* and *utu* (revenge). *Mana* was all-important and any insult or slight, however trivial, demanded retribution.

Intertribal warfare was frequent, either for *utu* or for more desirable land. The Maori man reveled in fighting and excelled in hand-to-hand combat, for which he fashioned weapons. He did not use throwing spears. Instead, he used the *taiaha,* a sort of wooden broadsword about five feet long with a blade for cutting and a hilt sharpened for thrusting. The *taiaha* was wielded with two hands. For even closer combat the Maori warrior used a *patu* and a *mere,* clubs about the length of a man's forearm. They were made either of wood, whalebone, or the very hard greenstone.

Before engaging in battle warriors would perform a *haka*. While it has the appearance of a war dance, the *haka* was really a limbering-up exercise, much like a boxer uses to limber up before the start of a fight. Today the *haka* is a popular item in Maori concerts and is often performed as a symbol of New Zealand by sports teams competing overseas.

For clothing and baskets the Maori used the leaves of native flax. They were stripped and dried and woven into cloaks or rolled into long tubes to make skirts (*piupiu*). The chiefs' cloaks were decorated with the feathers of birds.

The Maori developed a distinctive style of wood carving, which he used lavishly. All Polynesians carved in wood but seldom reached the artistic standard of the Maori. The design was not haphazardly chosen; each had a meaning and each carving told a story. The human figure was distorted and grotesque so as not to offend the gods by making a true image of a human being.

For a time it appeared that the carver's art would be lost, but the government established the Maori Arts and Crafts Institute at Rotorua, which has enabled exponents of carving to continue the tradition.

Tattooing was traditional to the early Maori. As a sign of status the warrior was heavily tattooed on cheeks, nose, and forehead in an intricate design of whorls. Women, too, were tattooed, but mainly on the chin (*moko*). It was a painful process. The skin was cut, not pricked, with a chisel and coloring was rubbed into the wound. Tattooing has long died out, but the designs are now painted on to the face for performances at Maori concerts.

Pride, Dignity, Intelligence

The basis for the integration of the Maori into European society was laid when the Treaty of Waitangi was signed by 45 Maori chiefs in the Bay of Islands on February 6, 1840. In essence, it recognized that the chiefs' lands belonged to the Maori and stated that any land they would be willing to sell would be sold only through the British Crown, which implied that the Crown was concerned with saving the Maoris from being cheated in private land deals.

The principles were laudable, but of course the treaty did not work. Representatives of the Crown wanted to buy the land for next to nothing; four years after the treaty was signed the Crown abandoned its right of preemption, and settlers were doing their own buying on their own terms.

The stage was set for what was to become a period of bitterness and strife. The wars over the sale and confiscation of land dragged on from 1860 to 1872. The conflict was a series of skirmishes rather than a national war over an unbroken period; it did not completely involve both races. Some Maori tribes were, in fact, friendly to the government. Although land matters are still not fully resolved, land classified as Maori property totals about 4 million acres and is administered by Maori interests.

Songs, Dances, Oratory

At the personal level, cultural pride embraces preservation of ancestral land and traditional arts, including wood carving, weaving, and oratory. The Maori loved oratory almost as much as fighting, and to listen to a Maori elder speaking on a *marae* in Maori is to hear poetry, even if the words and meaning are not fully understood.

Double Heritage of Culture

From the early days there was a good deal of intermarriage between Maori and pakeha, which has intensified over the last three decades. One result has been a greater drawing together of the two races in a desire to foster their bicultural heritage. As Witi Ihimaera, well-known Maori author, says in his book *Maori:*

"Today, one in every twelve persons in New Zealand is of half or more Maori origin. In addition, the non-Maori population includes another 50,000 people who are part but less than half Maori. On top of this, it can be safely estimated that most New Zealand families have relatives with Maori blood and more than cursory contact with Maori people.

"In effect, most New Zealanders now have a double heritage of culture. Rather than maintain the division between Maori and pakeha, many New Zealanders now seek a compromise world where Maori culture has an equal place with pakeha culture in New Zealand, where New Zealand is as bi-cultural as they are.

"There has been, therefore, a growing identification of many New Zealanders with Maori culture. This identification has tended to contest the question of what, in fact, constitutes a Maori. Intermarriage has meant that today there are few, if any, full-blooded Maori in New Zealand. For present census purposes he is one who states that he has half or more Maori blood. By the same token, none other than verbal evidence is required to substantiate a claim to being a Maori, which means that a Maori is a Maori if he says he is.

"The usual visual evidence of a brown skin is no longer the sole criterion, and some Maori today have such non-racial characteristics as green eyes and red hair. Such has been the success of integration."

The Arts in New Zealand

In spite of the image of New Zealand as a generally sporty, outdoorsy nation, a majority of New Zealanders demand an increasing number of cultural services.

New Zealanders buy more recorded music per capita than any other country except Sweden. Surveys show that more than 80 percent of the adult population actively support the range of cultural activities which concern the Queen Elizabeth II Arts Council, the principal government body dealing with the arts.

While New Zealand's population is just over 3 million people, it counts 4,000 craft potters who earn part or all of their living from their craft, another 40,000 who make and sell some pots, and an equal number who study pottery at adult-education or higher education classes.

In towns with a population of more than 5,000, there is generally at least one amateur theater group, a craft center, public library, and a brass band or music group.

Information on the various arts activities occurring in and around different New Zealand cities and towns can be obtained from the visitors' bureau in each center.

The rise of New Zealand writers in all fields of fiction, drama, and poetry, the proliferation of strongly individual visual artists, the production of New Zealand feature films, the emergence of New Zealand composers and choreographers, the establishment of local television drama series featuring New Zealand writers, actors, and directors, and the growth of characteristic New Zealand rock music, has meant a flowering of activities which collectively have created greater interest than ever in the arts.

Major examples of Maori carving can be found in the large collections in the Auckland Museum and National Museum in Wellington, both of which include a larger meeting house (*whare nui*), and in museums in Gisborne, Napier, Nelson, Christchurch, Dunedin, Wanganui, Rotorua, Invercargill, New Plymouth, Te Awamutu, Hamilton, and Whakatane.

At the Maori Arts and Crafts Institute in Rotorua, visitors can watch young carvers learning the art under masters. Carving objects of nephrite jade (greenstone) and bone is also a long-standing tradition that is flourishing.

Theater

After the demise of the national professional company The New Zealand Players in 1960, six full-time professional theaters were gradually set up. Wellington's Downstage (1964), Auckland's Mercury Theatre (1968) and Theatre Corporate (1973), Christchurch's Court Theatre (1971), Fortune Theatre in Dunedin, and Centrepoint Theatre in Palmerston North (both 1974), are now backed up by cooperative theaters such as Circa and the Depot in Wellington and New Independent Theatre and Working Title in Auckland.

Films

After making only three feature films in the 10 years prior to 1975, the New Zealand film industry began to produce feature films at the average rate of three to four a year.

Music

The establishment of the New Zealand Symphony Orchestra in 1946 as a division of the public broadcasting organization gave impetus to local classical music making. The orchestra now gives more than 100 concerts a year with international and local guest conductors and soloists. Regional professional orchestras in Auckland, Wellington, Christchurch, and Dunedin present many local concerts.

After a troubled history in the 1960s, the New Zealand Opera Company ceased to function. Professional opera was revived in 1978 and has now been incorporated into the Mercury Theatre's annual repertoire.

Visual Arts

A network of 10 major public art galleries throughout the country from Auckland to Dunedin constantly show major exhibitions and smaller projects of New Zealand historical and contemporary art, while dozens of dealer galleries in the main centers have continuous shows by major and minor painters, usually for a fortnight at a time.

Recent growth in photography and print making has seen the establishment of several specialist galleries dealing in these media.

Crafts

As many as 4,000 registered craftspeople create ceramics, weaving, hand-made jewelry, and carved craft objects throughout New Zealand, but particularly in areas such as Coromandel and Nelson.

New Zealand is particularly strong in its creation of handcrafted ceramics, developing a plethora of individual styles from the original strong Japanese classical influence of visiting potters.

In woolcraft, wall hangings and rugs are a characteristic concern of New Zealand craftspeople. Jewelers are experimenting with indigenous materials such as bone, paua shell, and stone, which are also being used by carvers.

Writing

Among modern writers, Sylvia Ashton-Warner, with her educational interests, Janet Frame in her powerful explorations of the individual's mental universe, Maurice Shadbolt and Maurice Gee in personal sagas, and Witi Ihimaera and Keri Hulme reaching into Maori spirituality, have all explored parallel themes of the country's development through a largely biographical fiction.

Dance

The Royal New Zealand Ballet is one of the oldest professional performing arts organizations in New Zealand, having celebrated its 30th anniversary in 1984. In spite of having had its costume store burned out at one point, and being reduced to a handful of dancers through financial constraints at another, it has survived to present a lively mix of classical and contemporary, internationally and locally choreographed repertoire, which it tours regularly throughout New Zealand, in an average of 70 performances annually.

New Zealand's premier modern-dance company, Limbs, which is based in Auckland, has an equally large repertoire of New Zealander–choreographed dances, which it tours and expands each year.

NATIONAL PARKS

A Legacy of Grandeur

As early as the beginning of this century New Zealand began preserving some of its most outstanding natural assets: It now has ten national parks, totaling over 5¼ million acres (one-thirteenth of the total land area) and encompassing forests and valleys, mountains and glaciers, inland lakes and coastal bays. Three are in the North Island and seven in the South Island.

Overall administration is carried out by the National Parks Authority, although each park has its own controlling board. The objective, set out in an act of Parliament in 1952, is to preserve these areas in their natural state for the benefit and enjoyment of the public.

Inevitably, the tourist must visit or pass through some of these parks, as they contain many of New Zealand's most beautiful and unusual attractions.

Without exception, the parks suffer from the depredations of animals. There were no mammals indigenous to New Zealand and, misguidedly, the early settlers introduced deer, opossum, stoat, and weasel and, in the Mount Cook region, chamois and Himalayan thar. Having no natural enemies and finding the environment much to their liking, the immigrant species multiplied rapidly until they became menaces to the native vegetation and bird life. They still destroy the forest cover, resulting in erosion on steep slopes and flooding of rivers, while birds fall prey to stoats, weasels, and domestic cats that have run wild. Some of these have been declared noxious animals, but the nature of the terrain makes it almost impossible to implement an effective control program.

Tongariro National Park

The nucleus of Tongariro, New Zealand's first national park, was set aside in 1887 when a far-seeing Maori chief, Te Heuheu Tukino, gave the summits of three mountains to the government to avoid inevitable sale to Europeans. "They shall be," he said, "a sacred place of the Crown and a gift for ever from me and my people."

Almost in the center of the North Island, the park has extremes of climate and terrain, ranging from forest to desert-like areas and geothermal activity. This central upland plateau has as its most prominent land forms three volcanic peaks rising almost in a straight line from north to south: Mt. Tongariro (6,345 ft.), a series of mildly active craters; symmetrical Mt. Ngauruhoe (7,515 ft.), the most active volcano; and Mt. Ruapehu (9,175 ft.), the highest mountain in the North Island, with an intermittently active crater from which radiate small glaciers. The park has an area of nearly 171,000 acres.

Tongariro National Park is the most accessible and easily seen of all the national parks. It straddles two main highways between Lake Taupo and Wellington on the east and Wanganui and New Plymouth on the west. It can, in fact, be circumnavigated by road with continuous views of the mountains.

Tongariro is also the most used of the national parks. Although only the upper part of Mt. Ruapehu is coated with snow in the summer and fall, the lower slopes are heavily covered in winter and form the North Island's most popular skiing resort. Skiers come from as far as Auckland and Wellington. About 40 mountain clubs have provided buildings in an alpine village from which a system of chair lifts, T-bars, and tows take skiers higher up the slopes.

The Tourist Hotel Corporation (THC) Chateau Tongariro is conveniently placed close to the main highway.

Egmont National Park

The second to be established, Egmont National Park of 82,836 acres surrounds the symmetrical cone of Mt. Egmont (8,260 ft.) and dominates the extensive and fertile farming country of Taranaki. It is easily reached by good roads from the main highways and is popular for skiing and climbing. Three roads run up into the park: from New Plymouth to the North Egmont Chalet; from Stratford to the Stratford Mountain House and plateau; and from Hawera to Dawson Falls and the Dawson Falls Tourist Lodge.

Geologists consider that Egmont may have been active about 220 years ago, but it is now dormant and its dense rain forest helps control the watersheds of 31 rivers that radiate from its slopes. The Maori hold the peak to be sacred. Skiers and mountaineers respect it as an excellent training ground.

Urewera National Park

By tradition the home of the Tuhoe tribe ("the children of the mist"), Urewera National Park lies in a remote region between Rotorua and Wairoa, on the east coast, and at 495,000 acres is the third largest of New Zealand's national parks and the largest in the North Island. A maze of confusing watersheds, it is noted for its Maori history, for the size of its area of virgin forest, and for its lake, Waikaremoana ("sea of rippling waters"), a vast, star-shaped lake of intense blue water and countless bays and coves some 2,000 feet above sea level.

The heavily wooded ranges include forest typical of the original vegetation. So vast and unbroken are the forests that the traveler does not have to go far from roads and tracks before he feels that no one has been there before him.

Access to the park is by a highway linking Rotorua and Wairoa, but it is a slow, winding road which must be taken with care. There is no hotel, but there are camping facilities near the Wairoa end of the lake.

Mount Cook National Park

The area of Mt. Cook National Park (172,739 acres) is not large by New Zealand standards, but its essence and quality are determined by the height and sheerness of the ranges and by the size and length of the glaciers, the great valleys they have gouged, and the rock debris they have spread. Waving tussocks, blue-green lakes fed by glacier water, tawny rocks and glistening snow add to the grace and breadth of the scene. The park is linked to Westland National Park by the ice-covered chain of the Main Divide of the Southern Alps.

The park is dominated by Mt. Cook, at 12,349 ft. New Zealand's highest mountain, and clustered around it are 17 peaks over 10,000 ft. The area has been a training ground for many mountaineers who have represented New Zealand in the Antarctic, the Andes, and the Himalayas.

The Alps were pushed up late in New Zealand's geological history, and have been sculpted into their present form by glaciers and streams. The degree of glaciation is outstanding high. There are scores of glaciers within the park, but the most impressive are the Tasman (18 miles), the Murchison (11 miles), the Hooker (7 miles), and the Mueller (8 miles).

An exciting sightseeing event is a skiplane flight with a landing at about 7,500 feet on the vast snowfield at the head of one of the glaciers.

Accommodation is available at the THC Hermitage complex almost at the foot of Mt. Cook. Although the Hermitage and Glencoe Lodge are at 2,500 ft., snow does not cover the ground except occasionally in winter, and no special warm clothing is needed.

The Hermitage is roughly halfway between Christchurch and Queenstown, and is reached by road or the regular services of Mount Cook Airlines.

Mount Aspiring National Park

South of Mt. Cook, Mt. Aspiring National Park is wild and rugged and visited mainly by enthusiastic hikers and hunters. The boundaries of its 680,000 acres extend along a 100-mile front, and its width is seldom more than 20 miles, but it effectively divides the eastern side of the South Island from the West Coast. The Haast Pass road to the West Coast traces the park's northern tip.

Like other South Island parks, Mt. Aspiring consists of glaciers and rocky mountains, thick bush, river flats and gorges, waterfalls and passes. It has some rivers so accessible that families may camp on the flats, and others so rough and inaccessible that only hardy hunters or hikers can reach them.

The park derives its name from its dominant feature, Mt. Aspiring, which rises to 9,931 ft. It is a distinctive peak, sheer and icy and rising to a needle point, not unlike Switzerland's Matterhorn.

The mountains may be comfortably seen across the lake from Wanaka, where the THC runs a well-appointed hotel. There are also motels.

Wanaka is reached by an alternative route from Mt. Cook to Queenstown, where the traveler turns off at a right angle at Tarras, reaching Queenstown through Wanaka and over the Crown Range. Wanaka is passed in the course of, or can be the starting point for, the journey through the Haast Pass to the west coast.

Fiordland National Park

Fiordland National Park is the grandest and largest of all—over 3 million acres, virtually untouched and in some places unexplored. It is larger than the total area of the other nine parks and one of the largest in the world. Its western boundary is a shoreline intended by countless fiords and bays. So difficult of access is the land that it was here as recently as 1948 that a small colony of *Notornis* (*takahe* in Maori), a swamp bird thought to be extinct, was rediscovered. It is also the only place in New Zealand where wapiti are established in the wild.

Fiordland has a wealth of history covering nearly two centuries and a great variety of people, from navigators, sealers, and whalers to explorers, surveyors, and miners. After rounding the southern point of the South Island on his first voyage, Captain Cook sailed *Endeavour* in March 1770 past the west-coast sounds but could not make harbor. At one place "dusk" intervened and at another the weather was "doubtful"; accordingly he named the sounds Dusky Sound and Doubtful Sound. On this voyage Cook left a few names on the map but never a footprint on the land.

The highlight of Fiordland is Milford Sound, a 10-mile-long, narrow waterway biting into precipitous granite cliffs rising thousands of feet. Milford can be seen on a 1½-hour scenic flight from Queenstown or Te Anau or can be reached by road from Te Anau by a journey of 75 miles through exciting alpine scenery. The vastness of the sound is best appreciated from a launch cruise.

For those who enjoy hiking, the most rewarding way to explore Fiordland is on the three-day, 33-mile walk over Milford Track, with overnight stays at accommodation huts. The trace passes the Sutherland Falls which, at 1,904 ft., are among the highest in the world.

The gateway to Fiordland, either by road or by the Milford Track, is Te Anau on the shores of the lake of that name.

The THC runs a comfortable hotel at the head of Milford Sound, and at Te Anau there is the THC Te Anau Hotel as well as several well-appointed motor hotels and motels.

Westland National Park

Westland National Park is dominated by the mountains and the sea. Its eastern boundary is the main divide of the Southern Alps, and from the sea on the west come rains that feed the forest and glaciers. The park's 219,000 acres are a mixture of high, snow-clad peaks, steep glaciers, lush rain forest, deep gorges, and cattle-farming country.

Westland's glories are the thick, verdant rain forests, attractive even in the rain, the backdrop offered by the long line of high, snow-covered peaks, and lovely, unexpected lakes.

The Franz Josef and Fox glaciers, flowing from vast snow fields shadowed by peaks more than 9,000 ft. high, are among the largest glaciers in the temperate zone. They descend for seven and eight miles, respectively, past flanks of luxuriant bush to less than 1,000 feet above sea level and only ten miles from the sea.

By glacial standards the rate of flow is fast—1,000 feet an hour. The rate of flow varies according to the pressure of ice built up in the snow basins high in the mountains. The specific rate of flow varies in different parts of the glacier, like the current of a river. The ice surges over itself, breaking and grinding and being forced up into pressure ridges by the movement of the flow.

The boundaries of the park are skirted by the traveler driving along the West Coast between the western portal of the Haast Pass and Hokitika.

There are hotels and motels at the Franz Josef and Fox glaciers.

Arthur's Pass National Park

Arthur's Pass National Park comprises 243,000 acres and extends on both sides of the main divide of the Southern Alps between Canterbury and the west coast. Its scenery, climate, vegetation, and development reflect its spread over contrasting areas.

Easily accessible, the park attracts people to its river flats, its forests, and, in winter, its snowy mountains. The main transalpine railroad, with its 5¼-mile Otira tunnel, and the main transalpine highway take a large number of people through the park.

Only 93 miles by road from Christchurch, Arthur's Pass is the shortest overland route to the west coast and Hokitika, only 63 miles farther on. It is a popular skiing area in winter, and there are day excursions by road and rail from Christchurch.

The road over the pass can be closed by snowfall, floods, or landslides in winter, but it is open for most of the year. Farther north, the Lewis Pass has easier gradients and is less vulnerable to storms, but the scenery is less spectacular.

There is a small township, called Arthur's Pass, near the summit.

Nelson Lakes National Park

Nelson Lakes National Park is a very popular recreation area for New Zealanders. Nelson people used it as such long before it became a national park and a tradition of a holiday at Lake Rotoiti was well established. It is much used in this way today as there are excellent facilities for camping, boating, swimming, hiking, trout fishing, and hunting.

Comprising 141,127 acres, Nelson Lakes is predominantly a park of bush-clad mountains, quiet valleys, swift-flowing rivers and streams, the seven-mile long Lake Rotoroa, and five-mile long Lake Rotoiti. Forests here mark a stage in the transition of vegetation from the rain forests of the West Coast to the dry grasslands east of the main divide. The bush is principally beech forest.

Abel Tasman National Park

Just north of Nelson, Abel Tasman National Park, with only 47,373 acres, is the smallest of the parks. Much of it is coastline and outlying islands, and its unspoiled golden beaches make it popular with New Zealanders for camping holidays. Access is either by sea or by land, but there are no hotel or motel accommodations.

FISHING AND HUNTING

Trout, Marlin, Shark, Deer, and Thar

New Zealand has long been renowned for its outstanding trout and big-game fishing and for its hunting for deer, chamois, and thar. Even though the number of local anglers is increasing, the quality of trout fishing remains consistently high and big-game fishing still yields some excellent fish. Because of the rugged landscape animals can be difficult to locate and the use of a guide is recommended.

Fantastic Trout Fishing

By overseas standards New Zealand is underfished. Its innumerable fast-flowing rivers and streams of clear mountain water and cold, clear lakes proved an ideal environment for the brown trout ova introduced and hatched in 1869 and the rainbow trout ova brought from Russian River, California, in 1877. Both species bred swiftly and were subsequently liberated throughout the country.

Fishery management by national and local wildlife authorities has maintained these qualities through sound conservation and hatching methods, and size and quality of trout are, in many cases, even improving.

So fast do trout grow in New Zealand that they rarely reach maturity until 14 inches long. In fact, all trout under this length must be returned to the water.

As an instance of this rapid growth, rainbow fingerlings weighing less than half an ounce each (forty to the pound) were liberated in 1981 in Lake Tarawera. When taken by anglers nine months later they weighed an average of 3½ to 4 pounds. Some grew 7 pounds in sixteen months.

27

The wildlife authorities estimate that each year about 700 tons of trout are taken by anglers from Lake Taupo alone, the average weight being 4.4 pounds.

A check taken a year or two ago indicated that about 6,000 anglers visited New Zealand and caught about 14,000 trout, or better than two trout per angler—better still when it is realized that most fishers returned unwanted trout to the water alive. These 14,000 trout at a conservative estimate weighed 14 tons, which proves that the claim "tons of trout" is no exaggeration.

For seven years Rotorua conducted a trout fishing competition for one week each year. Over the seven weeks, 5,018 trout were weighed and found to total 17,654 pounds—nearly 8 tons, or over a ton of trout each week. The fish averaged 3.52 pounds.

Lake Tarawera has a reputation for producing more 10-pound trout than any other lake in the world. The summer average, when the fish are feeding deep in this lake, is 5 pounds; but in May and June, when the trout come up from the deep and gather at the stream mouths to spawn, fly fishing comes into its own. In May and June of a recent year fish of 9 to 10 pounds were caught almost daily. The biggest was a female weighing 13.2 pounds.

The average brown trout passing through a fish trap on a Lake Taupo spawning stream weighs 6.71 pounds. In the South Island, browns average 2 to 3 pounds, although in such rivers as the Mataura, Clinton, and Hollyford, 5-pound fish are commonly caught.

The daily limit per angler differs slightly from one district to another but is usually eight to ten trout a day, and trout under 14 inches long must be returned alive to the water. Rainbow trout taken in Lake Rotorua average from 2 to 4 pounds and in Lake Taupo from $3\frac{1}{2}$ to 6 pounds. In Lake Tarawera the rainbow trout average 5 pounds, but weights of 8 to 10 pounds are not uncommon.

Whopper after Whopper

The main fishing areas of New Zealand are the lake systems of the North Island, including Lakes Rotorua and Taupo. Here the quarry is the rainbow and the usual method of fishing is with wet fly (streamer).

Most streams flowing into lakes are designated for fly fishing only, and sinking lines with lure-type flies are most favored. Trolling is popular and most productive, and during the summer floating lines are used for rising trout. Spinning is also popular.

In the South Island the brown trout is predominant and most plentiful in the southern lakes, rivers and streams of Southland. It is taken mainly by dry fly, or nymph. Rainbows and landlocked salmon as well as sea-run browns are also taken in the southern lakes. Here, spinning, trolling, and wet fly are used with success. Rainbows and browns average 2 to $2\frac{1}{4}$ pounds but run to 5 pounds in some areas. Rainbows of 10 pounds can be found and 11-pound browns are not unusual.

Although several areas, notably Lakes Taupo and Rotorua, are open all the year round, the main season is from October to the end of April (in some districts as late as the end of June).

Most serious anglers who try to avoid the January vacation period find that dry fly fishing is good in October, December, February, and March. Wet fly fishing in lakes, mainly at stream mouths, is good from October to December and in February–March and is excellent in rivers when trout start their spawning runs, from April through September. Trolling and spinning are both good from October through March.

Fishing licenses are reasonably priced. In most areas day licenses cost $8.50 and, for a week, average $21.50. A tourist license is available to visiting anglers at a cost of $66. This allows the holder to fish anywhere in New Zealand for one month (with the exception of one Maori-owned lake where an additional day license is needed). In the Rotorua/Taupo area daily licenses are $6 and weekly licenses are $16.

Accommodations in the popular fishing areas are good, with many hotels and motels of high standard at Rotorua, Taupo, Turangi, Wanaka, Queenstown, Te Anau, Gore, and Invercargill. There are also fishing lodges at Lakes Okataina, Tarawera, Rotorua, Makarora, and at Turangi. Camping and caravan sites are plentiful, and many small country hotels in fishing areas make the angler especially welcome. The roads to most fishing areas are good.

Scattered throughout the most popular areas are 100 or more professional guides. They provide all equipment needed, including first-class rods, lines, and reels. Most have boats, from fiberglass 14-footers to 50-foot overnight launches, and many have passenger-licensed automobiles.

The average price of a top fly fishing guide supplying all equipment and vehicle to reach streams is $300 to $400 per day. Trolling guides operating 15-ft. boats with canopy and two motors run a daily average of $300 to $400. Fifty-ft. launches charter at $500 to $700 a day, or $50 to $70 an hour, plus $100 for overnight trips, plus meals, and can sleep up to six, who share that rate.

BIG Big-Game Fishing

The coastal waters of New Zealand teem with fish of all descriptions. Those that can be regarded as big game are broadbill swordfish; blue, black, and striped marlin; mako, thresher, and hammerhead shark; yellowtail (or kingfish, as it is known locally); and tuna. Excellent light-tackle sport can be enjoyed with smaller varieties such as bonito, skipjack, and the famous *kahawai* (sea trout).

Big game fish are found mostly on the eastern coast of the North Island between North Cape and Cape Runaway in an area warmed by the Pacific tropical current. Here are found the big game fishing bases of Whangaroa, Bay of Islands, Tutukaka, Mercury Bay, Tauranga, Mayor Island, and Whakatane. All are less than 200 miles from Auckland and visitors with limited time can fly to them by amphibian aircraft.

New Zealand's big-game-fishing grounds are world famous for producing big fish; in fact, striped marlin, the most prolific of all marlin in these waters, average around 250 pounds. Black marlin average from 400 to 600 pounds: a 976-pound black marlin held the world record from 1926 to 1953. Pacific blue marlin range from 300 to 600 pounds.

New Zealand all-tackle records are: broadbill, 673 pounds; black marlin, 976 pounds; blue marlin, 1,017 pounds; striped marlin, 465 pounds; yellowtail, 111 pounds; thresher shark, 922 pounds; tiger shark, 947 pounds; hammerhead shark, 460 pounds; mako shark, 1,000 pounds; yellowfin tuna, 168 pounds; bluefin tuna, 519 pounds.

The trend in New Zealand fishing circles is to lighter tackle. For many years most charter boats used 130-pound (and heavier) line but most now carry 80-pound line, while enthusiastic sportspeople are taking records on lines of 50, 30, and even 20 pounds.

Top of the light-tackle fish are the yellowfin tuna, which run from 40 to 100 pounds. Second are the yellowtail closely followed by the skipjack, bonito, and *kahawai*. The *kahawai* is in fact eagerly sought by fishers using fly rods and fly lure. Seasoned trout anglers say that *kahawai* fights better, pound for pound, than trout.

Kahawai is also the popular bait fish used by big game fishers when trolling or drifting for marlin and shark. It is found in huge schools, often up to an acre in extent. At times, *kahawai* can be seen "boiling" on the surface at all points of the compass.

Charter boats are available at all the big-game bases mentioned. Most are fitted with two chairs, outriggers, and ship-to-shore radio. Most boats are operated by owner-skippers who are fully conversant with the fishing and other conditions in their areas. Costs are around $650 a day.

Membership of any of the big-game-fishing clubs runs from $5 to $10 annually. It entitles one to use all facilities and to enjoy the general conviviality of such clubs everywhere. Visitors are made especially welcome. The season is from mid-January through April. Smaller game fishing, especially for *kahawai,* is good all year.

Hunting

The daily rate is $350 for one hunter and $450 for two, plus equipment and food, and an hourly rate of $600 for a helicopter (3 seats) to locate game and gain access. World-class trophy animals—chamois, thar, and deer (red, sika, and fallow)—can be hunted from lodges on game-management areas, where all hunting is controlled. Trophies of each species are guaranteed. The average price for each animal starts at $2,000 and increases on a point system, depending on the rating in the world record books.

Interested hunters can obtain lists of all guides from the Fishing and Hunting Officer, New Zealand Government Travel Office, Private Bag, Rotorua.

THE NORTH ISLAND

"The Fish of Maui"

by
JOHN P. CAMPBELL

New Zealand is a land of startling scenic contrasts. The North Island has its weird geysers and bubbling mudpools, where underground steam sizzles through cracks in the ground as if from Nature's pressure cooker. Huge clouds of steam billow from the vast underground reservoir, which is now tapped to provide power for electricity.

The South Island has the dramatically impressive beauty of its Alps and fiords, its forests and rivers, and its enchanting lakeland. But the North Island has its share of rolling pastureland and verdant forest-clad hills, so easy on the eye and restful to the senses.

In ancient Maori mythology the North Island is *Te Ika a Maui* ("the fish of Maui"). While fishing with his brothers, Maui, who was descended from the gods and had magical powers, fished the North Island from the sea. Disobeying his orders not to touch the fish, his brothers gnawed at it to assuage their hunger, causing the fish to writhe and thresh about and giving the island an undulating or mountainous landscape.

Auckland (pronounced "Orkland"), the arrival point for most visitors, divides the bulk of the island from the long peninsula of Northland. Being nearer to the equator than the remainder of New Zealand, Northland has a subtropical climate, with superlative seascapes and uncluttered beaches. It is a dairying region, with some sheep farms, but also has large citrus and tropical fruit orchards. It is the birthplace of New Zealand as a nation,

31

for it was here that the Maoris signed the Treaty of Waitangi, acknowledging British rule.

Most visitors travel south from Auckland through the center of the island to Rotorua to see the thermal activity, and to meet Maori people in one of their principal homes. A detour of some 46 miles is necessary to visit the Glow-worm Grotto of the Waitomo Caves (definitely not to be missed), but this is always included on organized tours and is easy to visit either in a rented car, or by coach.

Wherever you travel in the North Island you'll pass through dairying and sheep-raising country, and it begins soon after you leave Auckland. On the road you'll notice a number of large stainless-steel tankers, some with trailers. They are not carrying gas or oil, but milk. These tankers collect milk from the farms every day and take it to factories, which make butter, cheese, dried milk powder, and other dairy products. One of the largest of these, a tall, gleaming modern building, is passed at Te Rapa just before reaching Hamilton, which stands on the banks of the Waikato River and is New Zealand's largest inland city.

To the left lies Tauranga, the Bay of Plenty and Poverty Bay on the east coast; to the right New Plymouth and Taranaki on the western bulge.

"An Endless Golf Course"

Beyond Hamilton you pass through some of the most fertile farming land in New Zealand. The rolling pastures and grass-covered hills are incredibly green and dotted with fat, white woolly sheep—they appear like mushrooms in the distance—and sleek dairy cows. The countryside looks like an endless golf course, so immaculately kept are the pastures. They always draw comment, and coach drivers often joke that "as soon as they upgrade the local golf course they are going to turn it into a farm."

The lush fields result from scientific farming. High quality grasses and clovers are sown, but the soil still needs additional fertilizer. Superphosphate, occasionally mixed with other ingredients, is spread annually, and often twice a year. This once laborious task is now done from the air—"aerial topdressing" it is called. This has become a fine art. Aircraft can now land, load a ton of superphosphate, and be airborne again within one minute. Only by aerial topdressing can much of New Zealand's hill country be kept fertile. The chances are that you'll see aerial topdressing being done as you travel.

Abruptly leaving farmland behind, the road enters thick bush and climbs over the Mamaku Range. This magnificent stand of native forest remains just as it was hundreds of years ago. As you peer through the tangled undergrowth, and admire the graceful trees climbing from the deep valleys, you cannot help wondering how the Maoris first found their way through it. You'll also understand why people still get lost in it, and why animals introduced to New Zealand, such as deer, pigs and opossums, which have no natural predators, multiply so prolifically and have been declared noxious animals.

Rotorua is the center of a hot thermal belt which begins in the Bay of Plenty some 40 miles to the east and continues to Tongariro National Park. Rotorua's thermal area, though vigorously active, is concentrated, and rather surprisingly, surrounded by rich green farms.

It was not always so. Until comparatively recent times the land, consisting to a large degree of volcanic ash and pumice, would grow little but scrub, but scientists discovered that the addition of small quantities of cobalt would make the soil productive. Topdressings of this and superphosphate have resulted in the development of highly intensive farming. The landscape has been transformed from a dull brown to a deep green.

World's Largest Human-Made Forest

It was also found that the pumice and volcanic soil supported pine trees, which mature here in 20 to 25 years, much faster than in other countries. The farming of these trees for lumber and pulp is now one of New Zealand's largest industries. Near Rotorua is the Kaingaroa Forest; 364,000 acres of pines, claimed to be the largest human-made forest in the world. There are other large forests at nearby Kinleith.

The trees are husbanded and harvested much like other crops. Replanting programs are followed, and the government maintains a Forest Research Institute at Rotorua. All New Zealand newspapers, and many in Australia, are printed on newsprint made at a large plant at Kawerau, a few miles from Rotorua. Understandably, the plant makes use of natural underground stream for some of its power. You'll see the fringe of the forest as you drive from Rotorua to Wairakei and Taupo, and pass through towering avenues of pines.

Fire is a constant danger, and in the dry summer months fire watchers are stationed in hilltop observation towers, and aerial inspections carried out. In the forests large roadside signs indicate the present degree of fire danger. Thoughtful people do not throw cigarette butts out the automobile or coach windows. One cautionary sign says: "Chaperone your cigarette— don't let it go out alone."

If time presses, you can fly from Rotorua to Wellington or Christchurch, or even to Mount Cook and Queenstown, but the road journey south is full of interest.

Only 56 miles (90km) from Rotorua is Taupo, on the northern shores on the lake of that name. Once little more than a sleepy village catering mainly for anglers (the lake is famous for the quantity and size of its trout) and summer holiday makers, Taupo is today a thriving modern town. It owes its prosperity to the development of farming and the growth of forestry.

Entering the town you descend an incline and cross a narrow bridge over sluice gates. This is the beginning of the long Waikato River, which flows out of the lake. Here, unlike the muddy river seen on the journey from Auckland, the waters are crystal-clear with an icy blue-green tinge, for they flow from the vast snowfields and glaciers at the opposite end of the lake.

In spite of its commercial activity, Taupo is still a mecca for anglers. More than 700 tons of trout, mainly rainbow, are taken from the lake each year!

The road follows the eastern shores of the lake for 32 miles (45.5km) to Turangi at the southern end. At Waitahanui, where a stream flows into the lake, you'll probably see a score or more anglers standing waist-high in the water, and almost shoulder to shoulder. At this particularly productive point, the congestion is known as the picket fence.

The road then winds through a narrow gorge, thought to have been formed by an earthquake, and climbs to a plateau, at the end of which is an especially beautiful vista of the lake and the sacred island of Motutaiko, a Maori burial ground. On a fine day the lake is colored in pastel shades, as if a rainbow had been laid on the waters.

Like Taupo, Turangi was once a sleepy trout-fishing village, but it is now the center of a large hydroelectric development nearing completion.

Hard-to-Pronounce Mountains

Within a few miles you enter the boundaries of the Tongariro National Park, with its three mountains—Ruapehu, Ngauruhoe and Tongariro. To the right, the road follows the western slopes to the Chateau, the North Island's most popular skiing resort, but the more direct route to Wellington is to the left. Some delightful forested valleys with tumbling mountain streams are passed before a long plateau is reached. This is known as the Desert Road, but it is nothing like a conventional desert. Overshadowed by three mountains and swept by winds, the area is arid and grows nothing but scruffy tussock in its pumice soil, although pine plantations are now being established. Anyone familiar with true desert would object to the description, but to New Zealanders, accustomed to grass-covered land, it is a barren wasteland. Near the center of the plateau the road is 3,600 ft. above sea level, and is occasionally blocked by snow in winter. Waiouru, at the southern end, is the North Island's main military base.

Hill-Country Farming

Green pastures soon appear again, but the terrain is steep and rugged—a good example of what New Zealanders describe as "hill country farming." The hills were once covered with thick forest, which was burnt off and replaced with good grasses and clovers. Sheep clamber up the steep slopes like mountain goats.

Slowly, the hills give way to rolling pastures, and finally to an extensive plain which slopes from the mountain ranges to the sea. It is an area of concentrated sheep farming and dairying, and once again the large number of sheep in the fields demonstrates the fertility of the land.

Just past Waikanae, some 40 miles (64.4km) from Wellington, there are fine views to the right of Kapiti Island off the coast. Once a stronghold of the infamous Maori chief Te Rauparaha, it is now a bird sanctuary. The land which appears, rising from the sea as you follow the coast to enter the suburbs of Wellington, is the northern tip of the South Island.

Most visitors tend to follow this central route and omit the delightful areas of the Bay of Plenty and Hawke's Bay on the eastern coast, and Taranaki on the west coast, because of the additional traveling time required. If time is not an important factor, it is a good plan to travel through the center of the island on the way south, and to return to Auckland from Wellington along the eastern or western coast.

In Hawke's Bay, Hastings and Napier are reached in one day by road or in 2 hours by air. The area is one of the largest vegetable and fruit producing regions in the country, and Napier is a delightful seaside city. From Napier one can travel through mountain passes to Taupo and Rotorua, or go up the east coast to Gisborne and through to Tauranga, in the Bay of Plenty, from which it is an easy drive to either Rotorua or Auckland.

The west coast route passes through the river city of Wanganui and on to New Plymouth, nestling beneath the slopes of Mount Egmont in Taranaki. The Glow-worm Grotto at Waitomo Caves lies close beside the main road to Auckland.

AUCKLAND

Rome was built on seven hills, Auckland on seven or more extinct volcanoes. Auckland is New Zealand's largest city, with a population of over 800,000. Situated on a narrow isthmus, it separates two seas, the Pacific Ocean and the Tasman Sea, and two harbors, the Waitemata and the Manukau.

Dominating the Waitemata Harbor ("Sea of Sparkling Waters") is Rangitoto Island, a long, three-humped, former volcanic island, whose shape never changes from whatever angle it is viewed.

Like parts of the United States, Auckland was bought for a song. History records that 3,000 acres of land were purchased from the Maori for $110 in cash, 50 blankets, 20 pairs of trousers, 20 shirts, 100 yards of cloth, 10 waistcoats, 10 caps, 20 hatchets, a bag of sugar, a bag of flour, 10 iron pots, 4 casks of tobacco, and a box of pipes.

A large population and an abundance of flat land gradually drew industry to Auckland, which is today New Zealand's largest industrial and commercial center. Thoughtful planning has, however, prevented most of the newer factories from becoming unsightly blotches and the new homes from being too stereotyped.

The growth of industry called for more labor, and, seeking opportunities for employment and education, thousands of Pacific Islanders, who also hold New Zealand citizenship, have flocked to Auckland. From the Cook Islands, Tonga, Western Samoa, the Tokelau Islands and from Niue Island they came, to make Auckland the largest Polynesian city in the world.

Unlike the Europeans who settled earlier, the Polynesians have tended to retain their own culture and customs and to live in their own communities. On Sundays especially you will see the women in long skirts and flowered straw hats, and the men in neat suits with white shirt and tie going to their own churches. Walk the length of Karangahape Road, to the north of the business center of the city, and you'll rub shoulders with as many Polynesians as Europeans.

They are mostly a happy, carefree people, but some have yet to adjust to the European way of life. They tend to congregate with their own compatriots, and some of the hotel bars have identified with them by painting their exteriors in the brilliant colors the Polynesians love, particularly reds and purples.

Queen Street: Narrow Valley Floor

Some New Zealanders consider that Auckland is humid in summer. There is some truth in this, but the humidity is nothing like as enervating as the humidity of New York, and there is usually the relief of a sea breeze.

Most of the principal hotels are close to Queen Street, the main street, which runs along a narrow valley floor, with side streets climbing off it like herring bones. Queen Street is a series of small shops, interspersed with larger department stores and some interesting arcades. One of the largest is the Downtown Shopping Centre (opposite the chief post office at the bottom of Queen Street), which has 70 shops under one roof, including a duty-free shop.

Almost opposite is the Old Auckland Customhouse at the corner of Customs and Albert Streets, where the architecture of the 1880s has been

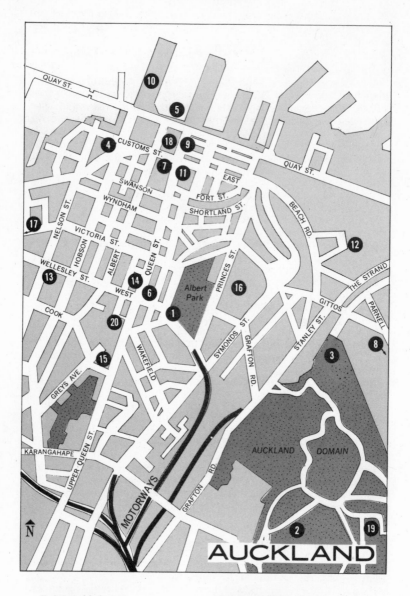

Points of Interest
1) Art Gallery
2) Botanical Gardens
3) Carlaw Park (Rugby League)
4) City Markets
5) Ferry Terminal
6) "246" Queen Street
7) Old Customhouse
8) Parnell Village Shopping Center
9) Post Office
10) Princes Wharf
11) Queen's Arcade Shopping Center
12) Railroad Station
13) St. Matthews Church
14) Strand Arcade
15) Auckland Visitors Bureau
16) University
17) Victoria Park Market
18) Downtown Airlines Terminal and
    Shopping Center
19) War Memorial Museum
20) Aotea Center

preserved and craft shops added. Just up Queen Street from the chief post office and also on the left is Queens Arcade, a recently refurbished area with 45 shops.

At 128 Queen Street is the Plaza Shopping Centre, which has a selection of specialty stores but has an emphasis on food services. At the Gourmet Food Gallery numerous stalls offer Mexican, Indonesian, Turkish, and French fare, together with roasts, fish and chips, an ice cream parlor, and a coffee shop. Just across the street is the C.M.L. Mall, catering to clothing, shoes, and fabrics, as well as caneware and costume jewelry.

Aucklanders are proud of their harbor bridge which links the city with the North Shore (a popular residential area and the main outlet to the north), even though they flippantly refer to it as the Coathanger. Previously the only link was by ferry or a long journey by road. Opened in 1959, the bridge is 3,348 ft. long, and its 800 ft. navigation span rises 142 ft. above the water. Within ten years the traffic flow had trebled, and extra lanes had to be to added to each side. It now has eight lanes.

Auckland War Memorial Museum

In the Auckland Domain, a large expanse of parkland and sportsfield, a short taxi or bus ride from downtown Auckland, is the Auckland War Memorial Museum. It is a memorial to the dead of two World Wars and is noted for its outstanding masterpieces of Maori art. The great carved house Hotunui and the only surviving Maori war canoe are centerpieces to a large display of Maori art and culture. The displays also cover New Zealand's natural history, including its bird life—particularly the extinct giant Moa bird.

Victoria Park Market

Victoria Park Market has transformed a former garbage treatment plant site into an attractive marketplace thronged with visitors every day of the week—a sort of high-quality flea market. A wide range of specialty shops sell prepared food, fresh fruit and vegetables, books, health foods, arts and crafts, clothing, ceramics and pottery, and just about everything else. There are four food outlets and an international food hall. It is about three kilometers from the city center and an inexpensive taxi ride.

Mount Eden

The 643-ft. symmetrical cone of an extinct volcano is Mt. Eden, some four kilometers from the city. The road spirals up the slopes to the summit, from which there is a complete circle of panoramic views of the city and outlying areas. From here one can look at two oceans with a turn of the head; on one side the Tasman Sea, on the other the Pacific Ocean. A table shows the direction and distances of the main cities of the world. Just below the lip is the deep red lava crater, fringed by grass, where sheep graze placidly.

One Tree Hill

This hill, 6 kilometers from downtown, catches the eye from the city, with its single tree and a 70-ft. obelisk honoring Sir John Logan Campbell, "the father of Auckland." On the crest of the hill is the Auckland Observatory. Like Mt. Eden, it was formerly a Maori fortified village.

Parnell Rose Garden and Village

Famous for its rose gardens and profusion of blooms in season (November), this sight is only 2 kilometers from the city.

Parnell Village, a couple of miles from the city, should not be missed. Here, an imaginative developer has transformed what was formerly a rather run-down part of Auckland into a delightful replica of early colonial days—not merely as a tourist attraction but as an attractive collection of shops.

Kelly Tarlton's Underwater World

Another Auckland highlight is Kelly Tarlton's Underwater World, which is far from a routine aquarium. The impression of actually being an underwater diver is strong as one takes the 8-minute trip on a conveyor through a 40-foot-long tunnel lined with acrylic windows. Over 30 species of fish, including sharks and stingrays, swim beside and above you in a natural environment. There are also fish pools and a 12-minute audiovisual show. The complex is opposite Orakei Wharf, on a bus route and close to the city.

Greenstone Factories

Greenstone, a type of jade, is distinctive to New Zealand and was widely used by the Maori to make weapons and ornaments. It is so hard that it has to be cut with diamond saws. It may be seen being cut and fashioned into modern ornaments at the factory of Greenstone Distributors Limited, 26 Honan Place, Avondale (8 kilometers outside Auckland), and at Finnegan's Paua and Greenstone Factory, corner of Gundry and Ophir Streets, Newton (five minutes by taxi from downtown).

Zoological Gardens

By overseas standards the Auckland zoo is not outstanding, but New Zealand's unique bird, the kiwi, can be seen in a special nocturnal house. The kiwi forages for food only at night, and the house is lit to resemble its native habitat.

Museum of Transport and Technology

Don't let this forbidding title put you off. This is a fascinating collection of equipment and machines that have now largely disappeared, including a working tramway, a railway, vintage cars and carriages, and wartime guns and aircraft. It also contains the remains of what was probably the second aircraft to fly. A New Zealander, Robert Pearse, designed and built an aircraft, which he twice flew in March 1904, just three months after the Wright brothers made the world's first powered flight. There is still argument whether Pearse did, in fact, fly first. Ancient vehicles have been painstakingly restored, and mounted on rails are old trolley cars and railroad locomotives. The camera and telephone exhibits are outstanding. If you grew up in the 1920s and 1930s you'll feel a pang of nostalgia to see the old type of gas pumps still bearing names like "Voco," and "Super Plume Ethyl" and even five-gallon cans labeled "Texaco" and "Shell." In another part of the museum about a mile away memories of World War II are revived by a Lancaster bomber, one of the type which carried out the daring raid on the Moehne, Eder and Sorpe dams in the Ruhr. Nearby are a Kittyhawk and a Vampire jet.

Aotea Center

The $9.5 million Aotea Center, a regional center for entertainment and conventions, opposite the Town Hall, opens in late 1988. In pleasant, landscaped surroundings, the center will have a 2,300-seat theater, a 250-seat restaurant, a lounge bar, and attractive foyers.

Vineyards

The Henderson area is renowned for its vineyards. They began in the 1890s when an immigrant from Lebanon, Assid Abraham Corban, brought with him a 300-year-old tradition in wine making and viticulture. Today, there are dozens of vineyards in a compact area, from large corporation enterprises to small individual holdings. A tour of some of the vineyards to taste the local product on the site is full of enjoyment.

NORTHLAND

"The winterless north" is how residents describe the long peninsula pointing north from Auckland. (Remember that seasons are reversed in the southern hemisphere). The claim is not strictly true, but the region is subtropical, and certainly warmer in winter than other parts of New Zealand. It is a productive dairying area and also contains New Zealand's only oil refinery, at Marsden Point.

Northland is often bypassed, as it is time consuming to travel. Even though the route is circular, it takes six or seven days if sufficient time is allowed for sightseeing. Yet it repays a visit. Even just three days will allow a visit to the most interesting area, the Bay of Islands.

In pre-European times much of the land was covered with a unique tree, the kauri. Of huge size, it is branchless for much of its length, and was therefore especially favored by the early whalers for masts and spars. The Maoris made canoes more than 100 ft. long from it. And the Europeans plundered it—a tragedy, as it is a slow-growing tree and takes a thousand years to reach full maturity. Today, the remaining forests are rigidly protected. There are three stands where the kauri may be seen in all its magnificence—the Waipoua State Forest and Trounson Park on the western side, and Puketi State Forest, near Waitangi, in the east. Waipoua State Forest has the greatest kauri of all—Tane Mahuta ("God of the Forest")—167 ft. tall and 14 ft. thick, with the lowest branches 60 ft. from the ground, and an estimated age of 1,200 years.

Through splits in its bark the tree exudes a gum which runs down the trunk and into the ground. It hardens into solid lumps of amber-colored, clear resin, which is today used for carved ornaments. In the latter part of the last century, however, it was much used for making varnishes, and thousands of Yugoslavs came to New Zealand as gum diggers. They dug for the gum in the ground and scaled the straight trunks to extract it from the branch forks. Modern synthetics replaced the gum, and many of the Yugoslavs became absorbed into other occupations or became grape-growers and wine-makers, a calling they still follow.

A little more than halfway up the narrow peninsula on the east coast is the Bay of Islands—a large semicircular indentation serrated by many bays and beaches, as if some giant sea monster had bitten into the coast with a mouth of jagged teeth. Within the bay are some 150 islands—the exact number is a matter of dispute.

This is the birthplace of modern New Zealand history. It was here that the Treaty of Waitangi, establishing British rule, was signed on February 6, 1840. Waitangi Day is observed as New Zealand's National Day, and a colorful ceremony is always held on the sweeping lawn outside the Treaty House, now a historical reserve. It was here, too, that Christianity was first introduced to the Maori. On Christmas Day 1814 the Rev. Samuel Marsden conducted the first Christian service to be held in the country.

Farther north on the west coast is the long stretch of Ninety Mile Beach (actually only 64 miles), and further up on the northernmost tip of New Zealand, Cape Reinga.

Between December and April marlin and shark appear off the eastern coast, and two points share popularity with other places farther south for big game fishing.

Exploring Northland

Traveling up the east coast, your objective will probably be the Bay of Islands, but pause to try the thermal springs at Waiwera, which means "hot water," and see the busy city of Whangarei. Here the Clapham Clock Museum in Lower John Street is world-renowned for its collection of clocks, and should not be missed.

In the Bay of Islands, Paihia, close to the Treaty House, and Russell stand on opposite sides of the bay. There are regular launch services connecting them, but vehicles have to be punted across a stretch of water. Because of its wider range of accommodations Paihia has become the holiday center.

Russell, once known as Kororareka, is redolent with evidence of early history. It was once known as the hellhole of the Pacific, when in the early 1800s whaling ships began calling for provisions. They traded with the Maoris with muskets and liquor, and brawling was commonplace. Nevertheless, after the signing of the Treaty of Waitangi it became New Zealand's first capital and was renamed Russell, but in 1841 the seat of government was moved to Auckland.

Russell still maintains an old-world charm. Dominating the waterfront is what is known as Pompallier House, a graceful Colonial-style building which could almost have come from the deep South of the United States. It is commonly thought of as the home of Bishop Pompalier, a Frenchman and the first Roman Catholic bishop of the Southwest Pacific, who arrived in 1838 to establish the first Roman Catholic mission. Actually, he never lived in it but in a building which has long disappeared. The present building bears no resemblance to the original two-storey structure made of rammed earth that was used to house the mission's printing presses. They produced several religious booklets printed in Maori. After the mission moved to Auckland it was used as a tannery for a time, but then sold to a local official, who transformed it into a fine residence. It was subsequently acquired by the government, and the Historic Places Trust has turned it into a museum, which contains a number of interesting exhibits.

Outstanding sidetrips from Russell (or Paihia) are cruises to outlying islands by launch (formerly known as "Fullers Cream Trip") or by the motor-powered large *Tiger Lily* catamaran. The big thrill is a Piercy Island turnaround, with its famous "hole in the rock." Here the sea surges through a funnel-like hole about 30 ft. long, 50 ft. high, and 40 ft. wide, and, with masterly maneuvering, the catamaran is edged slowly through the gap. Both the catamaran and the launch have comfortable cabins, hostess services, and bars. Take your lunch or order one when buying your ticket.

Across the bay is Waitangi, the birthplace of New Zealand history. On a grassy lawn sloping to the sea the Treaty of Waitangi was signed.

The Treaty House is fascinating. It was built as a home by the newly-appointed British resident, James Busby, in 1833, and is typical of the type of home favored by the more prosperous of the early settlers. In addition to a collection of historic items, it contains the first piano brought to New Zealand. In front of the house a kauri flagstaff marks the place where the treaty was signed.

Of greater interest, however, is a Maori meeting house *(whare runanga)* which is unusual in that it contains carvings from many different tribes; a meeting house usually has only the carvings of its own tribe. Beside it is a 117-ft. war canoe built for the 1940 centennial celebrations. It is made in three jointed sections, cut from huge trees.

Relics from the Bottom

Two miles (3.2km) beyond the Treaty House is Mount Bledisloe (376 ft.), from which there are wide views of the Bay of Islands.

It is worth pausing near the Waitangi Bridge to see the Museum of Shipwrecks, housed in an old wooden ship sitting on the river bottom. Here a collection of what diver Kelly Tarlton has brought up from the sea bed is exhibited.

Just a few miles away is the township of Kerikeri, one of the first mission stations. It is a prolific citrus-growing area, but a rich soil and kind climate also favor other subtropical fruits.

Almost on the river bank is the Mission House, the oldest building in New Zealand, which has been carefully restored, and the old Stone Store, still a store and in part a museum.

It's a full-day bus trip to New Zealand's northernmost tip, Cape Reinga. Part of the route is along the hard sand of Ninety Mile Beach and then up a shallow river bed. From the lighthouse at the cape you can watch the Pacific Ocean meet the Tasman Sea in a flurry of angry water. It was from here, the Maoris believed, that the spirits of the dead departed on their journey back to their Pacific homeland, Hawaiki.

Ninety Mile Beach is famous in New Zealand as a source of the toheroa, a type of clam which grows up to 6 inches long and from which is made a delicious green soup. Unfortunately, this is hard to get, as restrictions have been imposed to conserve the toheroa beds, which were being depleted. More plentiful, however, is the tuatua, a similar but smaller type of clam, which is also mouth-watering.

The return to Auckland from the Bay of Islands is usually made down the west coast and through the Waipoua State Kauri Forest.

Waitomo Caves

Resist the temptation to say, "when you've seen one cave you've seen them all." Certainly the Waitomo Caves have stalactites and stalagmites like so many others, but they also have a feature which is unique—the Glowworm Grotto. Neither words nor pictures can capture the beauty and the atmosphere. A visit is a remarkable experience.

With a guide, you descend to a deep cavern through which flows a quiet, sluggish stream. You are warned to keep silent, because the glowworms extinguish their lights at noise. At a landing you take your place in a flat-bottomed boat, the electric light is extinguished, and the guide slowly pulls the boat by wires around a cornice and into a vaulted cavern festooned with thousands and thousands of pinpricks of light—tiny individually, but collectively strong enough for you to see your companions in the darkness. Except for the occasional sound of dripping water the silence is complete. Above and around you myriads of glowworms shine their steady blue-green light, the dark, still waters glistening with their reflections like a star-studded carpet.

The Waitomo glowworm is an unusual species, quite unlike the glowworms and fireflies seen in other countries. While most other glowworms shine their lights as a mating lure, the Waitomo glowworm lights up to attract food. The hungrier it is, the stronger the light. Visitors are able to see the glowworms at close hand in what is called the "demonstration chamber" close to the grotto. Guided tours of the cave run every hour from 9 A.M. to 4 P.M., (0813) 88–228, for $6.

The Waitomo Caves are 126 miles (203km) from Auckland and 46 miles (74km) off the main route to Rotorua. Such is their beauty that they are always included in an itinerary unless lack of time makes it impossible. It is possible to include the caves in a tour of other parts of the region, and they are also a convenient stopover point if one is driving from Auckland to New Plymouth or Rotorua.

Rotorua

Rotorua is an area of contradictions. Gentle scenic beauty and violent thermal activity exist side by side. It has long been regarded as New Zealand's prime attraction, both for overseas visitors and New Zealanders themselves.

It has also remained one of the traditional homes of the Maori people, and it is the best place to meet them and to gain an insight into their philosophy and culture. But don't expect to see them living in native reservations or around the streets in their native costumes. They are completely integrated into modern society and live, dress, and work the same way as Europeans. Far from there being any segregation, they mingle freely and on equal terms. But to entertain the visitor they don their traditional costumes to give Maori concerts at night. Few are fulltime entertainers; most of the men and women you see performing hold regular jobs as secretaries, shop assistants, radiographers, technicians, or clerks. The woman you see performing intricate and graceful dance movements may serve you your breakfast in the morning.

(A reminder: Maori is pronounced *Mau-ree,* not *May-ori.* Not that offense is taken at a mispronunciation, but you might as well give a good impression by saying it right.)

Rotorua, 149 miles (239.8km) south of Auckland, once relied on tourism, but forestry and farming are now major industries, and the city's population has grown to over 47,000. Don't be concerned at the smell as you approach. Because of the underground thermal activity there is frequently a pungent odor of hydrogen sulphide: the locals sometimes jocularly refer to it as Sulphur City. But the natural gas is harmless, and one quickly becomes accustomed to the smell.

For many years Rotorua was a popular spa resort, and many went there to bathe in the mineral waters. Modern medicine tends to discount the curative power of the waters, but it does not dispute their value in relieving minor aches and pains. There is nothing more relaxing than soaking in a hot thermal pool after a day's sightseeing. You'll sleep soundly. The Polynesian Pools near the center of the city have a variety of baths, and many hotels and motels have their own pools, as do some private homes.

Don't be alarmed by discolorations on the water taps and fittings. They are not dirty. Chemicals in the water tend to tarnish certain metals; in fact, you can often identify "Rotorua money" by the dullness of the silver coins.

The Hot-Water Belt

Rotorua sits on a huge bed of hot water and steam. You'll see it seeping from banks and culverts, from gutters beside the sidewalks, from clumps of bushes, and even from the middle of flower beds. It is not uncommon to see hot and cold pools side by side. In fact, hot earth is one of the natural hazards in the main golf course.

Residents of the "hot water belt" take full advantage of this by sinking a bore and harnessing the steam to heat their homes and pools, and even do some of their cooking. You'll often see thin pipes rising from gardens to let off surplus steam.

Rotorua is at the southern end of the 32-square-mile lake of that name. Unfortunately, the name is not as evocative as it sounds. It simply means "second lake" (*roto* means lake and *rua* means second). When the migrating Maori canoe *Arawa* landed on the east coast an exploring party moved inland. They found a large lake, Rotoiti ("first lake"), and then a larger lake, Rotorua.

The Arawa tribe settled in the Rotorua area, and it is still their homeland.

In the center of Lake Rotorua is Mokoia Island, the scene of the greatest of Maori legends, a love story that ended happily. Against the wishes of her parents, a Maori maid, Hinemoa, who lived on the shores of the lake, fell in love with a young chief, Tutanekai, who lived on the island. Her efforts to sail to her lover in a canoe were foiled, and night after night she listened to the sounds of Tutanekai playing his flute to guide her. Finally she could stand it no longer and under the cover of darkness slipped into the water and swam the long mile to the island, guided by the sounds of the flute. Exhausted and cold, she dragged herself up the beach and sank into a natural thermal bath, which bears the name Hinemoa's Pool.

Tutanekai, who had retired for the night, was unable to sleep and sent a slave to a cold spring near the pool for a calabash of water. Disguising her voice, Hinemoa asked the slave for a drink of water. He passed the calabash, which she promptly smashed. He returned to Tutanekai and reported the insult, and Tutanekai seized his club and rushed to the pool to challenge the stranger, only to find his beloved. He placed his cloak around her and embraced her and led her to his hut, and they were married and lived happily ever after.

The love story is still related in song, and two streets in the city have been named after the lovers.

As Maori names are used so extensively in Rotorua, it is helpful to know how to cope with these seemingly tongue-twisting words. Break the words into syllables, give each vowel its full value, and remember that every word must end in a vowel and that "wh" sounds like an "f". For example, Whakarewarewa breaks down into *Whaka-rewa-rewa,* Tutanekai into *Tu-tan-e-kai.* Hinemoa into *Hine-moa,* Whakaue into *Wha-cow-e,* Ohinemutu into *O-hine-mutu,* and Tamatekapua into *Tama-te-ka-pua.*

Apart from its thermal activity, Rotorua is also a popular area for trout fishing in the nearby lakes and streams.

Exploring Rotorua

No area in New Zealand has such a wide variety of sightseeing. Two or three days, or more if possible, should be spent here to enjoy all the area offers. Excursions are well organized and inexpensive.

Information and brochures on sightseeing and tours may be obtained from the New Zealand Travel Office, 67 Fenton Street, 85–179; the Rotorua Promotions and Development Society, Box 90, 84–126, or individual sightseeing operators.

Whakarewarewa

Commonly shortened to Whaka. It is essential that the tourist visit this weird thermal area, only a couple of miles from the city center. There are two entrances, but it is recommended that you enter through the replica of a fortified Maori village (a *pa*) beside the main highway. An ornately carved gateway straddles the thick palisades to the village. The two figures at the gateway depict the famous lovers, Hinemoa and Tutanekai.

From the entrance a well-kept path bordered by native shrubs twists its way through outcrops of steam and boiling mud and silica terraces. Tiny geysers hiss beside you, and spouts of boiling mud leap from the mud lakes like jumping frogs. In the center of the area is Pohutu Geyser, New Zealand's largest, which plays to about 100 ft., often for long periods. Its activity is heralded by the "Prince of Wales Feathers", three jets which play spasmodically to a height of 40 ft. Below all this feverish activity a small cold stream flows placidly along the floor of the valley. Just before you leave the thermal area you pass a number of Maori graves, concrete-encased above the ground because of the earth's heat, and reach a collection of hot pools in which the Maoris who live nearby still cook their food. Meat and vegetables are placed in a woven flax basket and immersed in the boiling water, or in a wooden or concrete box set into the earth to trap the steam; a sort of natural pressure cooker.

Maori Arts and Crafts Institute

This is situated beside the main entrance to the Whakarewarewa thermal area and should not be missed. It is not a museum, but a living preservation of Maori art and culture. As the Maori acquired the European way of life there was a danger that the Maori arts would disappear; so, with government assistance, the institute was formed some 20 years ago.

For a three-year course of training under a master carver, the school accepts four students of less than 18 years of age, chosen from four Maori tribes. They are paid the same wages as apprentice carpenters. Some of their smaller carvings can be purchased, but the larger pieces are destined to replace deteriorating carvings at meeting houses in various parts of the country.

Women are not permitted to carve by Maori ethics, but at the institute they demonstrate traditional Maori weaving with flax, the making of *piupiu* skirts (flax leaves rolled into tight tubes), and basket and mat making. Instructors now go all over New Zealand to teach. The institute is funded by the fees paid to enter Whakarewarewa. There is a kiwi house near the institute where live kiwis may be seen.

Government Gardens

It was left to the government to beautify Rotorua in the early days (there were not enough local residents to meet the cost), which it did by forming what are still known as the Government Gardens, close to the center of the city, facing Hinemaru Street. Rotorua was then much favored as a spa resort, and, in an effort to emulate the elegance of European resorts, a large and incongruous Elizabethan-style bathhouse was built, and surrounded with lawns and flower gardens.

It is no longer used as such and contains an art gallery, museum, and restaurant. The formal flower gardens are delightful, and, surprisingly, steam often rises from stone cairns in the middle of them. There are also well-kept greens for playing lawn bowls and croquet in summer.

Some 3,000 temperate to tropical orchids, 300 of which will be blooming at any one time, are displayed in the Fleur International Orchid Garden in the Government Gardens. Among them are plants valued at up to $5,000 and new locally-developed hybrids. The orchids are displayed in two large plant houses heated by natural underground steam. Landscaped pathways lead through tropical foliage and native bush with waterfalls and streams. Adjacent is a free-flight parrot aviary. Hours are from 10 A.M. to 10 P.M. daily.

Polynesian Pools

Rotorua's natural thermal waters can be enjoyed at the Polynesian Pools in the Government Gardens. There are two public pools, one for adults and one for children, and 20 well-appointed private pools, all fed by the soft alkaline mineral waters of nearby Rachael Spring. There are also the Priest and Radium Springs, with their eight pools of different temperatures, bubbling out of the pumice. This spring water is acidic, and is well-known for relieving arthritis and similar ailments.

Ohinemutu Maori Village

Ohinemutu is truly a Maori village in that only Maoris live there. But do not expect to find native huts; they live in European-style houses. Nevertheless, it is one of the most fascinating places in Rotorua. Although it is on the edge of the cold waters of the lake, the land is pitted with harmless little geysers, and steam rises from crevices. In the courtyard stands a bust of Queen Victoria, surrounded by four decorated pillars and shielded by a canopy decorated with Maori designs and carving.

Two buildings are of special interest. Almost on the shore of the lake is St. Faith's Anglican Church, built in Tudor style in 1910. You cannot escape a feeling of reverence as you enter. The layout is traditional, but the decorations are distinctly Maori. Rich Maori carving is everywhere— on the pews, the pulpit and the altar. Hymn books are in Maori.

As you approach the sacristy move to the right and sit in the front pew. Before you is a large window fronting the lake. On it is etched the figure of Christ—a Maori Christ wearing a chief's robe—at such an angle that he seems to be walking on the waters. Near the entrance to the church hang several historic military flags.

If you can, attend a service. To listen to the liquid and sonorous Maori language and the harmonious singing is an emotional experience. It is also an opportunity to mingle with the Maori people in their own environment.

Opposite the church is the Tamatekapua meeting house, an ornately carved building containing some venerated work dating from about 1800.

The house is named after the captain of the Arawa canoe, and the carved figures in the interior represent passengers in the canoe. The figure on the top of the center post is Ihenga, who claimed the hot lakes district for the Arawa people. Another figure represents Ngatoroirangi, the canoe's navigator and *tohunga* (priest).

Fleur Orchid House

The Fleur Orchid House in Hinemaru Street and backing into the Government Gardens is one of Rotorua's newest attractions. It contains hundreds of orchids. Some are raised locally, some are imported from overseas, and some are virtually priceless. The orchids are most tastefully displayed amid rockeries and ferns, and there is vivid greenery and color all the year round. The Fleur Orchid House (476–699) is open daily from 10 A.M. to 10 P.M., admission $4.

Kuirau Domain

Just a short stroll from the city is Kuirau Domain, a pleasantly grassed area which has the inevitable boiling mud pools, steam vents and small geysers. More unusually, it has a shallow pool of thermal water which is used as a foot bath. It does indeed invigorate tired feet.

Maori Concerts

A Maori concert is an unforgettable experience. Their original chants *(waiata)*, which usually describe the history and ancestry of the tribe, are monotonal, rather like a church litany, but they warmly embraced the European tone scale, giving to the melodies their own harmonic variations. Maori singing is truly sweet and rhythmic.

Maori concerts are given in full costume in most of the larger hotels, at the Maori Cultural Theater, the Tudor Towers in the Government Gardens and Ohinemutu. The THC Rotorua International Hotel and several others add spice by giving a Maori feast every evening, followed by a concert. For a reasonable charge nonguests can attend the meal and entertainment, but reservations are essential.

Pork, chicken, ham and vegetables are cooked in a *hangi* (oven) in the hotel grounds. A large hole is dug and partially filled with river stones which have been heated to a high temperature. Water is thrown on them to make steam, the food in flax baskets or other containers is placed on top, and covered with soil. That is the true Maori oven, but in Rotorua the natural superheated underground steam dispenses with the need for heating stones. The principle and effect are, however, the same. The food is taken into the concert area and eaten informally.

The concert always begins with the traditional Maori ceremony of welcome. Grimacing fearfully and brandishing a *taiaha* (a long club), a warrior from the host tribe advances to the visitors with a sprig of greenery. He places this at the feet of the leader of the visitors and cautiously retires. If the visiting leader picks up the greenery he comes in peace; if not, it is war. Needless to say, the sprig is always picked up at a concert. The host tribe then greets the visitors with a song of welcome—*Haere mai, Haere mai, Haere mai,* thrice welcome. The ceremony is held in respect, and guests are asked not to applaud.

So musical are the Maoris that they do nothing without singing. Lilting melodies accompany the graceful *poi* dances by the women as they deftly twist and twirl balls of plaited flax.

It is impossible not to feel the blood stirred by the war dance *(haka)* performed by the men. The chant is in a simple rhythm and the tempo is kept by stamping feet—the Maori did not use drums. Every part of the body is brought into action in a set routine, even to protruding and wagging the tongue. The *haka* was intended to strike fear into the hearts of the enemy, but was also a "limbering up" exercise for hand-to-hand battle.

The concert always ends with the traditional Maori song of farewell, "Now is the hour" *(Po ata rau)*. It is not strictly a Maori melody, but Maori and *pakeha* alike have adopted it as a traditional New Zealand song. They sing it first in Maori and then in English, and as its plaintive notes die it is impossible to escape a feeling of sadness at parting.

Waimangu Round-Trip

The Waimangu thermal valley gives a good idea of how the earth was formed. It contains both furious thermal activity and quiet bush with grass-covered slopes rising from placid pools. The main valley can be seen from a mini-coach on a half-day trip. An extension, which includes some walking, adds launch cruises on Lake Rotomahana, with its steaming cliffs, and Lake Tarawera, where you meet a bus for the return to Rotorua.

The Waimangu Valley was created by the violent eruption of Mount Tarawera in 1886. In the early hours of June 10 the northern peak blew up, splitting the range into a series of massive craters. The noise was heard hundreds of miles away. Ash and debris were strewn over 6,000 square miles, and the Maori villages of Te Wairoa, Te Ariki, and Moura were destroyed. Maori legend tells that a phantom canoe was seen in Lake Tarawera just before the eruption.

Among other things, the eruption destroyed the famous Pink and White Terraces, glittering staircases of silica, and the Waimangu Geyser, once the world's largest, which played to a height of 1,600 ft.

But other remarkable sights remain or were created. The Waimangu Cauldron occupies a crater formed by a later and milder eruption and is a boiling lake of about 10 acres. The flow at the outlet is more than a thousand gallons a minute. Above the lake rise the jagged Cathedral Rocks, red-tinted and gently breathing steam. Ruaumoko's Throat (he was the god of the underworld) has an atmosphere of suppressed unearthly violence. Roughly circular, the crater is the bed of a pale blue steaming lake of unknown depth which overflows periodically at a rate varying from 200 to 3,000 gallons a minute. At times the water recedes 50 ft. to uncover the beautiful white walls of the crater. Bird's Nest Terrace is aptly named, but has miniature geysers and a silica terrace formation. Surrounded by vegetation, the Warbrick Terraces are layers of orange, brown, black, white and green caused by algae and mineral deposits falling from the top platform.

Te Wairoa Buried Village

In contrast to geysers and hot mud pools, the Te Wairoa Buried Village is tranquil but interesting.

Once the starting point for the trip to the Pink and White Terraces, the village of Te Wairoa was buried under eight feet of ash in the eruption. It has now been partly excavated—a sort of miniature Pompeii. There are many interesting relics, but as one walks through the heavily grassed pastures fenced by tall poplar trees and English cherries it is hard to visualize the devastation which occurred.

Of special interest are the remains of a *tohunga's whare* (priest's house). The tohunga, who was reputed to be 110 years old, did not predict the

coming disaster and was therefore blamed for it by the tribe, who refused to allow him to be rescued from his buried house. After four days they relented. Incredibly, he was still alive, but died a few days later. Relics of the eruption are still being excavated and are on display in a museum, which also includes displays of kauri gum and polished New Zealand rocks.

Tikitere

Appropriately named Hell's Gate, Tikitere is an area of furiously bubbling pools and seething mud, including a mud waterfall. It is an eerie place, but intriguing.

Mount Tarawera Tours

When Mount Tarawera erupted it blew a 9¾-mile rift along almost its entire length, leaving a jagged chasm with walls up to 800 ft. high. From the air, it is an awesome sight, and there are helicopter and fixed-wing aircraft tours that include a circuit of the mountain and a flight across the crater as part of a scenic tour, which takes in the surrounding native forests and lakes, the vast pine forests, the Blue and Green Lakes and aerial views of the city. Some aircraft land on a strip at the summit of the mountain. Another way of viewing the crater is by a four-wheel-drive cruiser that travels from Rotorua up the side of the mountain to the summit.

Lake Okataina

Lake Okataina, 19 miles from Rotorua, must be one of the loveliest lakes in New Zealand. Steep hills, thickly clad in subtropical forest, enclose the blue-to-turquoise waters and delightful sandy beaches. The place is alive with native birds, and deer roam the forest. Of human habitation there is only a tourist lodge, a launch and runabouts for enjoying a cruise and for fishing, for the lake is renowned for the abundance and size of its rainbow trout.

The name means "place of laughing", but you are more likely to relax and absorb its serenity and beauty. The approach is impressively beautiful, through thick native forest and a tunnel of native fuschia, whose flowers form a red carpet on the roadway in the spring.

Trout Pools

Even if you don't catch trout you can see them at close quarters at Rainbow Springs and Paradise Valley Springs. Here they live a protected life in crystal-clear pools in native bush, gradually evolving from tiny fingerlings to 8- and 10-lb. monsters. In some springs the path is below the pool, one side of which has a thick plate-glass window, through which you can see the fish cavorting beneath the water. It is enthralling to watch the trout, like performing dolphins, leaping from the water to seize small pellets of meat held above the pool on the end of a stick. Rainbow Springs also has a kiwi house where a live kiwi may be seen.

Taniwha Springs

Taniwha Springs, 7 miles from Rotorua, has dozens of busy waterfalls, gushing springs, glittering sandsprings, and several trout pools set in native bush. A short climb takes you to an old Maori fortified village site. It takes its name from a legendary water monster, the "taniwha."

Skyline Skyrides

An outstanding attraction is Skyline Skyrides, just a few miles from Rotorua center. A 900-meter gondola lift, with a vertical rise of 200 meters, takes you up the slopes of Mt. Ngongotaha to a panoramic view and a restaurant and cafe. Descent can be by the gondola or a 1-km-long luge, or slide ride.

Agrodome

Even if you think you've seen enough sheep as you've traveled through New Zealand, a visit to the Agrodome, five miles from Rotorua, is well worthwhile. Here you can meet them at first hand and watch performing sheep take the center stage and show off their rich fleeces. Top-class shearers describe the characteristics of 19 different breeds and demonstrate shearing techniques. But the sheep dogs steal the show as they muster sheep into a holding pen, often without a bark being heard.

Heli-Jet Tours

A Heli-Jet tour is an adventure, but safe. It is an unusual combination of helicopter sightseeing and a ride in a jet boat. A helicopter takes you to the unspoiled Lake Rotokawau, nestling amid towering native forest and tree ferns. You step from the helicopter into a waiting jet boat and then speed at up to 50 mph over the lake before returning to the airport by the helicopter. The tour takes about 1½ hours.

Waiotapu

While much of the thermal activity at Rotorua is vigorous, the phenomena at Waiotapu are quieter, but beautifully colored. The area is 19 miles from Rotorua and is conveniently visited when driving from Rotorua to Wairakei and Taupo.

Wairakei

There is no settlement of Wairakei—just a comfortable Tourist Hotel Corporation hotel, a superb golf course, and a dramatic example of how man has harnessed Nature's vast underground heat for his own benefit. This is the site of the Wairakei Geothermal Steam Power Project, where scores of bores have been driven several thousand feet into the earth to tap huge underground reservoirs of super-heated steam, which is then piped to a powerhouse to make electricity. The steam drives turbines, which feed 192,600 kilowatts into the national supply.

You'll know when you approach Wairakei, 50 miles south of Rotorua. Huge clouds of steam pipes arch over the road, and a sign warns of a visibility hazard from drifting steam.

The complex is unusual, to say the least, and its like can be seen in few parts of the world. A roadside information center graphically demonstrates the project, and an impressive view of the steam field can be obtained from the crest of a hill behind the area.

Lake Taupo

Six miles beyond Wairakei lie Taupo and the lake. On the way, a detour should be made to view Huka Falls on the Waikato River. The falls are not particularly high, but they are spectacular. Compressed into a narrow rock channel, the river boils and surges before it gushes over a 35-ft. ledge into a maelstrom of white and green water.

Lake Taupo, New Zealand's largest lake, is 25 miles long and 17 miles wide and about 1,100 ft. above sea level. It is almost the geographical center of the North Island. The Maoris called it *Taupo Moana* (the Sea of Taupo).

To anglers throughout the world the name Taupo is synonymous with trout, for it is famous for the abundance and excellence of its fishing both in the lake and in the numerous rivers and streams flowing into it. It is said that over 700 tons of trout are taken from the lake each year! The average weight is 4½ lb., and 7- and 8-lb. fish are not uncommon. Charter boats are available for hire from the small natural harbor.

Until recent years the township of Taupo, at the northern end of the lake, was a sleepy village catering mainly for anglers and holidaymakers, but the development of farming and forestry have transformed it into a clean modern business town of some 13,000 people. It has also become a popular retirement place, with many fine homes.

From the lake's edge there are good views of the mountains in Tongariro National Park. Off the southeastern shore of the lake is the island of Motutaiko, an ancient Maori burial place and therefore sacred.

Tongariro National Park

The most popular national park in the North Island, Tongariro National Park, some 60 miles south of Taupo, encloses 175,000 acres of brown tussock plains and native forest. Dominating the park are three mildly active volcanoes—Mount Ruapehu (9,175 ft.); permanently snowcapped; Mount Ngauruhoe (7,515 ft.); and Mount Tongariro (6,458 ft.). Curiously, it is the lesser mountain which gives its name to the park. They huddle close together, as if for protection.

Ruapehu still has a steaming lake in its snow fringed crater. Ngauruhoe, an almost perfect cone, still sends up occasional puffs of steam; and Tongariro, which blew its top countless years ago, still has warm slopes in places.

The park is a tribute to Maori generosity and wisdom. In 1886, to avoid other tribal claims and the inevitable sale of the land to Europeans, Te Heuheu Tukino, hereditary chief of the Ngati Tuwharetoa tribe, gave the land to the government ("It shall be a sacred place of the Crown and a gift for ever from me and my people"). There is a succinct tribal proverb: *"Ko Tongariro te Maunga; ko Taupo te Moana; ko Te Heheu te Tangata"*—"Tongariro is the mountain; Taupo is the sea; Te Heuheu is the man".

There are many Maori legends about the mountains, but the most popular is that there were once more of them in the park, and all were in love with the womanly Mount Pihanga, to the north. They fought, and the vanquished were banished, but they could move only during the hours of darkness, and now remain in parts of the North Island where daylight touched them. One, Mount Taranaki, hurried westward, scouring the course of the Wanganui River as he went, and by daylight reached the position by the sea where he still stands.

From late spring through fall the mountains are bare of snow except for the upper slopes of Ruapehu, but in winter all are deeply snowcovered. Ruapehu is the North Island's most popular ski resort and has chairlifts and ski tows to the upper ski fields. Many ski and mountain clubs have huts here.

There are pleasant walks through the native bush, and at the National Park Headquarters there is a fine exhibit of the park's geology, flora and fauna. There is also a good golf course, and tennis courts.

Tauranga

Finding the Maoris of the east coast of the North Island hospitable, Captain Cook named the area the Bay of Plenty. In the production of dairy products, meat, and fruit, it is still a region of plenty. Its principal city and port is Tauranga, with a population of 48,000. Not far away is Maketu, the landing place of the *Arawa* canoe in the great migration from Hawaiki.

Tauranga's genial climate made it chiefly a retirement area, and center for holidays and big game fishing. Now its character is changing, but it has lost nothing of its charm. It is now a modern, thriving city, supported by the export of lumber from the man-made pine forests near Rotorua, 55 miles away, and farming.

Two narrow entrances open to a sheltered harbor. The city is on the western side, and opposite, at the tip of a peninsula, is Mount Maunganui, standing like a sentinel at the entrance. Sweeping beaches and good swimming make this a popular holiday resort. Off the coast is Mayor Island, the main big game fishing center.

Tuaranga and nearby Te Puke are the heart of New Zealand's kiwifruit industry. The area annually exports about a billon-and-a-half of the rich, furry, brown fruits.

On the main highway from Rotorua, four miles from Te Puke, a kiwifruit complex has been opened. The complex is recognizable for its four-and-a-half-story fiberglass kiwi slice. "Kiwi Karts" take visitors on tours of the office and coolstore complex, and a restaurant serves many dishes made with fresh kiwifruit.

Kiwifruit wines may be sampled at Preston's Winery on Belk Rd., off State Highway 27 (tel. 410–926), and Durham Light, a winery in Glen Lyon Place off Cropi Rd. (tel. 85–043).

Various birds may be seen at the Kati Kati Bird Gardens on the main highway to Auckland (tel. 490–912).

Gisborne

Because of its closeness to the International Date Line, Gisborne claims to be the most easterly city in the world, and the first on which the sun shines.

It was at Gisborne that Europeans first landed on New Zealand soil. Knowing that he must be near land, Captain Cook offered a gallon of rum to the first man to sight land, and promised that the part seen would be named after him. On October 7, 1769, Nicholas Young, a twelve-year-old cabin boy, sighted a headland, which was promptly named Young Nick's Head.

Two days later Cook led a party ashore at Kaiti Beach—the spot is marked with a memorial. A series of misunderstandings led to bloodshed, and Cook sailed away. He named the area Poverty Bay "because it afforded us no one thing we wanted."

Contrary to Cook's description, Poverty Bay is anything but poor, but a highly productive area for lambs, corn, vegetables, citrus fruit, grapes and wine.

Kaiti Hill Lookout

From the summit of Kaiti Hill there are splendid views of the city and the long sweep of the bay, including Young Nick's Head. At the foot of the hill is one of the largest Maori Meeting houses in New Zealand.

"Star of Canada" House

The bridge of a 7,280 ton ship in a city street! In 1912 the *Star of Canada* was wrecked on Kaiti Beach. The superstructure was salvaged and reconstructed as a house, which is now used as a private residence.

Napier

Napier is a phoenix city, risen from the ashes. Without warning on February 3, 1931, a severe earthquake shook the province of Hawke's Bay, and was felt further afield. Much of the city and many houses in the suburbs were flattened and fire ravaged a good deal of what remained. Hills crumbled and crevices opened in the roads. The Ahuriri lagoon was raised and over 8,000 acres of new land arose from the sea bed. Today, factories and the airport are on this new land.

Out of the chaos order was restored in a surprisingly short time. Napier was rebuilt as a modern city, and now has a population of 50,000.

Standing at the center of the wide sweep of Hawke's Bay, Napier's pride is the Marine Parade fronting the city. Lined for two miles with graceful Norfolk pines, it has beautiful sunken gardens, a dolphin pool, a concert auditorium, a roller skating rink and an aquarium.

On the parade stands the graceful bronze statue of Pania of the Reef. Maori legend has it that Pania, one of the Sea People, left them to live with her human lover, Karitoki. But she yielded to the constant calls of her people to return, and swam out to meet them. From the caverns of the sea they came to draw her down, keeping her forever from her lover. And so Pania sits, gazing forlornly out to the sea.

Exploring Napier

Regular sightseeing tours are run by Cox World Travel and also by taxi companies. Features at Napier are the formal botanic gardens and the lookout from Bluff Hills, affording panoramic views of the bay.

Cape Kidnappers Gannet Sanctuary

Cape Kidnappers, a cliff-faced promontory jutting into the sea at the southern end of Hawke's Bay, was named by Captain Cook because here the Maoris tried to kidnap his interpreter, a Tahitian boy.

Only recently has an overland route been opened to the gannet sanctuary. Twenty two miles (35.5km) from Napier, it is the world's only mainland gannet colony. At the cape visitors can obtain excellent views of the gannets, and walk quite close to the nesting birds. There are between 12,000 and 13,000 birds at the sanctuary in the height of the season, which is between November and February.

A fully-grown gannet weighs about 5 lb. and has a wing span of 5 ft. Eggs are laid in October, and take about six weeks to hatch. The chicks are fully fledged at 12 weeks and fly after 16 weeks. Migration of the chicks and dispersal of the adult birds occurs in February and March, and by April most birds have gone. Because of the rugged nature of the terrain, visits can be made only in special vehicles on tours run by Gannet Safaris.

Hastings

Thirteen miles (21km) south of Napier is Hastings, with a population of 51,000. There is friendly rivalry between the two cities; each has, for instance, its own daily newspaper.

It is a well-kept city, proud of its parks, gardens, and streets. Closer to the fertile sheep farming country of Hawke's Bay and to large vegetable and fruit farms, Hastings is more of a commercial center. There are a number of food processing plants, including Wattie's Canneries, which cans and quick-freezes huge quantities of vegetables and fruit. It is the largest and most complex plant of its kind in the southern hemisphere. Nearby meat-packing plants process about three million head of sheep and cattle annually.

Although most New Zealand wine is produced in the Auckland area, there are large vineyards near Hastings and Napier. The larger wineries, which welcome visitors, include Greenmeadows, a Catholic mission which is possibly New Zealand's oldest vineyard. It produces a variety of excellent table wines. Vidals Wines were founded in 1902 in converted racing stables; their wines are now well known and also sold in Australia. At nearby Havelock North, T.M.V. Wines runs the oldest commercial vineyard in the country. North of Napier, Glenvale Wines are one of the largest producers.

Hastings is the host city for two popular annual events: the Cherry Blossom Festival in October and the Highland Games at Easter, when the city resounds to the skirl of bagpipes and competitions are held in Highland dancing and sports.

New Plymouth

The perfect cone of Mount Egmont (8,260 ft.) dominates the province of Taranaki, which was also the Maori name for the mountain. It is a dormant, but not extinct, volcano. The ash from its ancient eruptions has made the land fertile, particularly for dairying, and Taranaki exports large quantities of cheese.

Below the northeastern slope of the mountain is the city of New Plymouth (population 43,000). Though a commercial center, it is a well-planned and attractive city.

It is also New Zealand's main hope for new sources of energy. Oil was found in the suburb of Moturoa as early as 1856, only seven years after the first discoveries in the United States, but the yields were small. Drilling in what is known as the Maui field, some distance off the coast, is raising hopes of a more bountiful supply. In 1962 natural gas was discovered at Kapuni and is now piped to various points of the North Island and provides considerable quantities of oil condensate for shipment to the oil refinery at Whangarei, north of Auckland.

Pukekura Park

Once a wasteland, this area was transformed by voluntary labor into a delightful park. One of the outstanding features is a small lake, surrounded by tree ferns, with the cone of Mount Egmont forming a perfect backdrop. At night an elaborate illuminated fountain plays in the lower of the park's two lakes and makes a colorful spectacle.

Adjoining Pukekura Park is Brooklands Park, where a natural amphitheater can seat over 16,000 people. A lake in front of the soundshell mirrors performances of drama, ballet, opera and music for the Festival of the Pines held in January and February.

Taranaki Museum

An excellent collection of early Maori sculpture and Maori carvings done with original stone tools may be seen in this museum, which also contains the stone anchor of the Tokomaru canoe, part of an early canoe fleet.

Pukeiti Rhododendron Trust

Any lover of flowers will be enthralled by this world-famous 900-acre park of rhododendrons and azaleas 18 miles (29km) from New Plymouth. It is at its best between September and November. There are about 900 species, all of which grow better in this climate than in their native habitat. Japanese nurserymen have been sending seedlings to the extensive nursery of Duncan & Davies; from which, after two years, they are shipped back, having grown as much as they would in five years in Japan.

Wanganui

One of New Zealand's oldest cities, Wanganui (population 38,000), stands near the mouth of the Wanganui River, which rises in the Tongariro National Park in the center of the North Island. The river was used as a canoe highway by the Maoris, and until recent years was navigated for more than 100 miles by launch, but this mode of transport gradually declined as roads were built.

The real beauty of the river is a 20-mile section upstream from Pipiriki, 49 miles (79km) from Wanganui, known as the Drop Scene. Here the river is confined to narrow, fern-clad gorges, where small waterfalls cascade down through the bush, and the water is churned into foam by rapids. The full-day trip is now done by jet boats.

Durie Hill

Panoramic views of the city and surrounding countryside can be obtained from the tower on Durie Hill (300 ft.). A road leads to the summit, which can also be reached by an elevator inside the hill.

Wanganui Museum

The Wanganui Museum has a good Maori collection, and New Zealand's first church organ, which has no keyboard and is operated like a pianola by a rotating cylinder.

Sarjeant Gallery

The Sarjeant Gallery displays a good selection of British and New Zealand painters of the nineteenth and twentieth centuries.

WELLINGTON

"Like San Francisco" say Californians when they survey the city from the surrounding hills. And it *is* rather like San Francisco. Its wide, circular

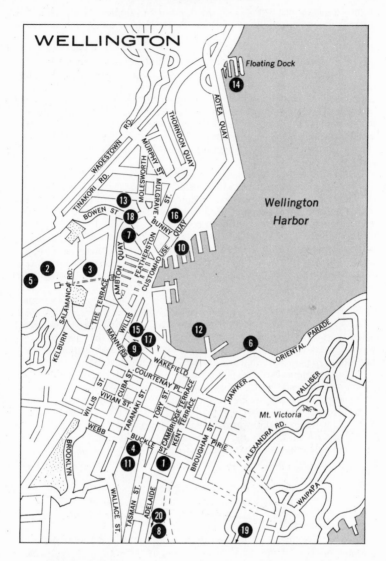

Points of Interest

1) Basin Reserve (Cricket and Soccer)
2) Botanical Gardens
3) Cable Car
4) Carillon & Hall of Memories
5) Carter Observatory
6) Freyberg Pool
7) Government Buildings
8) Government House
9) N.Z. Travel Office
10) Main Docks
11) National Art Gallery and Museum
12) Overseas Shipping Terminal
13) Parliament House
14) Picton Ferry Terminal
15) Post Office
16) Railway Station
17) Town Hall
18) War Memorial
19) Wellington Airport
20) Zoo

harbor lies in a basin of steep hills, the shops and offices cluster near the waterfront, and it even has a cable car! As the lights glow at night it resembles Hong Kong.

Wellington stands at the southwest tip of the North Island, and only a 20-mile stretch of water, Cook Strait, separates it from the northern tip of the South Island. The gap is bridged by 4,000 ton passenger-vehicle ferries which cross the strait frequently every day.

It is known as Windy Wellington. Cook Strait seems to funnel every breeze that blows and expand it into a wind. Most are gentle to moderate, but in the spring and fall they become strong. They are not unbearable, and at least they prevent air pollution. Other cities have a joke: "You can always identify a Wellingtonian because he grabs his hat when he rounds a corner."

Wellington is the capital city, and a large proportion of Wellingtonians work in government departments, whose head offices are here—rather like Washington, DC. Many national business concerns also have their head offices in Wellington, though there is a gradual migration to Auckland, where the factories are tending to concentrate.

The combined urban areas have a population of about 354,000, making it the second largest city. The number in the city boundaries is, however, much less, as there are large residential and light industrial areas in the adjoining Hutt Valley and Porirua basin. Lower Hutt and Upper Hutt are cities in their own right.

Wellington is justly proud of its magnificent harbor, a huge circular basin reached through a channel from Cook Strait and hemmed by steep hills. As the settlement grew from its small beginnings problems arose. There just wasn't enough flat land. The extension of the business areas was achieved by reclaiming land from the harbor. One of the main streets, Lambton Quay, is no longer a waterfront and is now about a quarter of a mile from the docks. From the waterside the hills rise so steeply that in some of the modern buildings you can enter a shop or office block at street level, ascend in an elevator to the second or third floors and exit at a door, still at street level.

Finding sites for homes also posed problems, and many houses climb dizzily up the hills, clinging to apparently sheer slopes. Many are built on stilts, and some even have their own small private cable cars.

There was only one way for the city to go—up. Wellington's two and three-story office and shop buildings are giving way to small skyscrapers. The height of the buildings was originally kept low, not because tall buildings were not originally needed, but as a precaution against possible earthquakes. Modern design and construction have, however, overcome the latter danger.

Named after the Duke of Wellington, who won the Battle of Waterloo between the British and the French, Wellington was settled by a company formed in England by Edward Gibbon Wakefield. The first ships arrived in 1840, and many of the streets are named after them or the British leaders of the day.

In 1865 Wellington became New Zealand's capital. It adopted as its motto *Suprema a Situ,* supreme by situation. In spite of Auckland's faster growth, it still holds proudly to that title. Certainly it is the geographical center of New Zealand.

Like Auckland, it has a population of Polynesians from the Pacific Islands, although in smaller numbers.

The best way to see Wellington is to take one of the half-day sightseeing coach tours run by Hammond's Sightseeing Tours, or the Wellington City Transport Corporation. The former leaves from the N.Z. Travel Office,

Mercer Street, (10 A.M. and 2 P.M.), and the latter from the Public Relations Office, opposite the Town Hall (2 P.M. daily).

Summit of Mount Victoria

Reached by a winding but well-made road through a residential area, the 558-ft. summit of Mount Victoria is the best known vantage point. From here the whole city and harbor seem to spread out like a gigantic relief map. To the west, the northern tip of the South Island can be seen on a clear day. In the roofed observation deck is a bronze bust of the Duke of Wellington staring austerely, not at the city named after him but, strangely enough, away from it. A short distance away is a stone cairn memorial to Rear Admiral Richard Byrd, an American explorer of the Antarctic who used New Zealand as a base for his expeditions. The stones embedded in the cement are from Antarctica.

Lambton Quay

Much of Wellington's main shopping area either follows the original shoreline or is built on land reclaimed from the harbor. Occasionally you will see plaques sunk into the pavement inscribed "Shoreline." For shopping, a stroll along Lambton Quay is absorbing, as many of the old buildings have been demolished and new ones erected, and for a mile there are intriguing little arcades, terminating at the city's tallest building, the Bank of New Zealand, at the junction of the quay and Willis Street. With its underground plaza, it's a little like New York's Rockefeller Center in miniature.

Parliament Buildings

Just above the Cenotaph, Wellington's war memorial, stand parliament buildings, the legislative center. The main marble buildings lack the towers which were originally intended but still present a solid dignity. At one end is a new circular building which looks remarkably like, and has therefore been christened, the Beehive. Inside, the government messengers will conduct you on a tour of the legislative offices.

Government Buildings

Below Parliament Buildings is one of the largest wooden buildings in the world. Consisting of 100,300 square feet, the government buildings, which house several departments, are a source of pride to Wellingtonians.

Alexander Turnbull Library

Just a short block up Bowen Street (behind the Cenotaph), a walk of 100 yards or so brings you to the Terrace (a long street parallel with Lambton Quay and the site of many of Wellington's tall commercial buildings). At Number 44 is the Alexander Turnbull Library. This is as much a museum as a library in that it contains a priceless collection of historic documents and many rare first editions. Included in the displays are the original signed sheets of the Treaty of Waitangi.

Old St. Paul's Cathedral

The Church of England's new cathedral faces Parliament Buildings on the corner of Hill and Molesworth Streets, but on Mulgrave Street, just a couple of blocks north, is Old St. Paul's Cathedral. This is one of the finest examples of a wooden church built in the early days. It was so much part of Wellington's history, and so beloved, that it is now preserved as a national shrine. The interior is exquisite.

Kelburn Lookout

A ride on the cable car should not be missed for the magnificent views of the city and harbor from the 480-ft. summit at Kelburn. The entrance to the city terminal is along a lane off Lambton Quay. Unlike the San Francisco cable cars, the car simply climbs a hill and then returns. It travels at a constant angle of about 15 degrees. Try to get seats on the left-hand side as the car ascends, and in front for the best views as the car descends. The car passes through three short tunnels and makes three intermediate stops before reaching the summit. The cars run frequently, and the return trip can be made after you have enjoyed the view.

Memorial Gates to the Second American Marine Division

As the Japanese began moving down the South Pacific, the Second American Marine Division made Wellington its headquarters. They were based at McKay's Crossing (a railroad crossing) near Paekakariki, some 30 miles north of Wellington on the main highway. From here they embarked for the bloodbath of Guadalcanal. The Memorial Gates, recalling the 17 months spent there by the division, stand at the entrance to the former camp.

Tramway Museum

Close by is a Tramway Museum, founded to preserve Wellington's trolley cars, now replaced by buses. The old trolley cars still run on a ¾-mile track in Queen Elizabeth Park.

Botanic Gardens and Lady Norwood Rose Garden

From a bus stop at the start of Lambton Quay (look for a bus with a "Karori" destination sign), a three-minute ride will take you to the entrance of the Botanic Gardens, 62 acres of native bush and exotic plants. Tulip Day especially (early October) demands a visit. Just a short distance down from the entrance to the gardens is the Lady Norwood Rose Garden, which is a profusion of blooms from summer thru fall. There is also a begonia house (open 10 A.M. to 4 P.M.).

National Museum and Art Gallery

On a mount overlooking the city and harbor stands the National Museum and National Art Gallery, fronted by the War Memorial Carillon Tower, with its Shrine of Remembrance. It is a landmark which can be seen from most parts of the city. The Maori section contains many authentic carvings and artifacts, including a meeting house which is considered to be the finest surviving example of its kind. There are some relics of Captain Cook, including the original figurehead from his ship *Resolution,* which he used on his second and third voyages to New Zealand. The colonial section shows early European life in New Zealand and features an "Early Wellington House" complete with furnishings. The museum is not directly serviced by public transport but is an inexpensive taxi ride from the city.

Directly opposite the city center is the dormitory seaside suburb of Eastbourne and to the northeast a four-lane motorway leads to the Hutt Valley, which is a mixture of light industry and pleasant suburban homes. Through the valley meanders the Hutt River.

First suburb to be reached, six miles out, is Petone, on the shores of the harbor, and it was here that the early settlers first landed. Just four miles farther on is the garden city of Lower Hutt, and some ten miles farther is Trentham, site of Wellington's main racecourse, leading to the city of Upper Hutt just beyond.

The route continues through farming areas, over the winding Rimutaka Hill and down to the Wairarapa Plains, one of the country's finest sheep-farming areas. The main town of Masterton (population about 20,000) is about 1½ hours' drive from Wellington.

Wellington's main highway north, however, branches to the left at Ngauranga, some five miles out of the city, climbs the steep Ngauranga Gorge and continues on a motorway until it descends to the sea on the west coast of the island at Paekakariki.

This is the start of "the Golden Coast" (or the Kapiti Coast) with its uncluttered and pleasant bathing beaches. Particularly popular with Wellingtonians is Paraparaumu Beach, some 35 miles out of the city and a developing retirement area on this coast.

Just off the beach is Kapiti Island, once a stronghold of the marauding Maori warrior Te Rauparaha and now a bird sanctuary.

In clear weather the northern tip of the South Island may be seen across Cook Strait to the south.

PRACTICAL INFORMATION FOR
THE NORTH ISLAND

ACCOMMODATIONS. New Zealand does not have "super luxury" hotels, but the better hotels are somewhat similar to the Hilton type, although styles vary. The average room rate ranges from NZ$85 to NZ$145, and motels from NZ$45 to NZ$60. The cities and scenic resorts are well served with good quality hotels and motels, but advance reservations, especially from Christmas through February, are advisable.

Many motels have fully equipped kitchens where you can cook your own meals; others have only tea and coffee-making facilities; some serve breakfast.

Some remote scenic areas are served by Tourist Hotel Corporation hotels (prefixed by the letters THC), which have high-quality accommodations, in the middle of mountains, lakes or fiords.

Auckland

Airport TraveLodge. Ascot and Kirkbride Rds.; (09) 275–1059. 253 rooms, high quality. Restaurants, bars, parking, pool.

Barrycourt Motel. 10–20 Gladstone Rd., Parnell; (09) 33–789. 126 rooms. Restaurant, bar.

Earls Court Motor Inn. 104 Gladstone Rd., Parnell; (09) 774–477. 25 serviced units, 2km (1¼ mi.) from city. Restaurant, bar.

Hyatt Kingsgate. Prince St. and Waterloo Quadrant; (09) 797–220. 327 rooms, restaurants, bars, Jacuzzis, jogging track. One of the most expensive Auckland hotels.

Mon Desir Hotel. 144 Hurstmere Rd., Takapuna (on the North Shore); (09) 495–139. 37 rooms, restaurant, bar pool, sauna.

Parkroyal Hotel. Customs St.; (09) 778–920. 184 rooms, restaurants, bars, refrigerators in rooms.

Quality Inn. 150 Anzac Ave.; (09) 798–509. 110 service units. Central location.

Quality Inn Rose Park. 100 Gladstone Rd., Parnell; (09) 773–619. 110 units. Restaurant, bar.

Regent of Auckland. Albert St., central; (09) 398–882. 332 rooms, restaurants, bars, parking, top quality.

Sheraton-Auckland Hotel. 85 Symonds St.; (09) 795–132. 410 rooms, 28 executive rooms. Top quality, central location, pool, bars, parking, sauna, spa, gym.

Takapuna Beach Motel. The Promenade, Takapuna; (09) 493–356. 28 units and studios with kitchens, bars; restaurant close by.

THC Auckland Airport Hotel. Cr. Ascott and Kirkbride Rds; (09) 275–7029. 160 rooms, restaurants, bars, parking.

TraveLodge. 96 Quay St.; (09) 770–349. 198 rooms, restaurant, bars, parking.

Vacation Hotel. 187 Campbell Rd.; (09) 664–179. 222 rooms, restaurant, bar, parking, 5 mi. from city.

White Heron Regency. 138 St. Stephen's Ave.; (09) 796–860. 75 rooms, restaurant, bar.

Bay of Islands (Paihia)

Autolodge Motor Inn. Marsden Rd.; (0885) 27–416. 50 rooms, restaurant, bar, parking.

Bushby Manor Motor Inn. Marsden Rd.; (0885) 27–527. 17 suites, nearby restaurant, pool, parking.

Casa Bella Motel. McMurray Rd.; (0885) 27–387. 16 units, parking.

Paihia Sands Motor Lodge. Marsden Rd.; (0885) 27–707. 8 units, restaurant, parking.

THC Waitangi. (0885) 27–411. 111 rooms, restaurants, bar, parking.

Gisborne

Quality Inn. Huxley and Tyndall rds., Box 113; (079) 84–109. 26 rooms, restaurant, bars.

Sandown Park Motor Hotel. Childers Rd.; (079) 84–134. 35 rooms, restaurant, bars.

Hamilton

Quality Inn Glenview. Ohaupo Rd.; (071) 436–049. 18 rooms, all facilities, restaurant, cocktail bar.

Quality Inn, Riverina Hotel. Grey St. across the river; (071) 69–049. 12 doubles, 31 singles, restaurant, cocktail bar.

Waikato Motor Hotel. Main highway at Te Rapa; (071) 494–959. 18 rooms, all facilities, restaurant, cocktail bar.

Hastings

Angus Inn Motor Hotel. Railway Rd.; 88–177. 58 rooms, restaurant, bar, parking, 5 minutes' walk to the city's center, adjacent to the racecourse.

Fantasyland Motels. Sylvan Rd.; 68–159. 19 rooms, private facilities but no restaurant or bars.

Napier

Ormilie Lodge. Omarunui Rd., (070) 445–774 Taradale. Nine deluxe units, restaurant, bar, parking.

Tennyson Motor Inn. Tennyson St.; (070) 53–373. 42 rooms, restaurant, bars, parking.

TraveLodge. Marine Parade; (070) 53–237. 60 rooms, restaurant, bars, parking.

New Plymouth

Devon Motor Lodge. 382 Devon St.; 86–149. 135 rooms, cabaret, pool, sauna, gym.

The Plymouth. Leach, Hobson, and Courtenay sts.; 80–589. 75 rooms, suites. Restaurants, bars, parking.

Quality Inn. 15 Bell Block; 70–558. Restaurant, bars, pool.

Westown Motor Hotel. Maratau St.; 87–697. Restaurant, bars, pool.

Rotorua

Geyserland Motor Hotel. Fenton St.; (073) 82–039. 76 rooms, restaurant, bars, thermal pool, massage facilities, golf course, pool.

Heritage Motor Inn. Fenton St.; (073) 477–686. 43 rooms, restaurant, bar, parking.

Kingsgate. Eruera St. (073) 477–677. Deluxe resort with 233 rooms, health center, some Jacuzzis, restaurants, bars, parking.

Muriaroha Lodge. 411 Old Taupo Rd., 2 miles from city center; (073) 88–136. Small, intimate, family-operated, exclusive hideaway on secluded grounds, beautifully landscaped. 7 suites and 2 bungalows furnished with antiques. Restaurant, bar, parking. Relatively expensive.

Okawa Bay Lake Resort. Lake Rotoiti, 12 miles from Rotorua on shores of Lake Rotoiti; phone Okere Falls 599 through long-distance operator. 44 rooms. Restaurant, bar, sauna, marina. Ideal for trout anglers. Relatively expensive.

Quality Inn. Fenton Park.; (073) 80–199. 74 rooms, restaurant, bars, heated pool.

Sheraton-Rotorua Hotel. Fenton St.; (073) 81–189. 144 rooms, restaurants, bars, roof-top pool, entertainment, spa, parking; top quality.

THC Rotorua Hotel. Froude St.; (073) 81–189. 150 units, restaurant, bars, refrigerators in rooms, thermal baths and pool.

TraveLodge Motor Inn. Eruera St.; (073) 81–174. 210 rooms, restaurant, bar, thermal pool.

There are also a large number of good quality motels, all rooms with private bath and toilet, some with thermal pools.

Taupo

Cascades Motor Lodge. Lake Terrace; (074) 83–774. 13 suites, 10 studio rooms, parking.

Huka Lodge. 2 miles from town on banks of Waikato River; (074) 85–791. 17 suites, exclusive and elegant.

Lane Cove Motor Inn. Lake Terrace; (074) 87–599. 15 suites, 2 luxury apartments, restaurant, bar, parking.

Manuels Motor Inn. Lake Terrace; (074) 85–110. Restaurant, bar, parking, pool, fishing, sauna.

Suncourt Motor Hotel. Northcroft St.; (074) 88–265. 52 units, restaurant, bar, parking.

Tui Oaks Motor Inn. Lake Terrace; (074) 88–305. 23 units, serviced rooms and units. Restaurants, bars, parking.

Tauranga

Otumoetai Hotel. Bureta Rd.; (075) 62–221. Near city, 80 rooms, restaurant, bar, parking.

Quality Inn. Girven Rd., Mt. Maunganui; (075) 55–089. 43 rooms, restaurant, bar, parking.

Tauranga Motor Inn. 15th Ave. and Turret. Rd.; (075) 85–041. 22 new units with thermal pools, cooking facilities.

Willow Park Motor Hotel. Willow St.; (075) 89–119. 44 rooms, restaurant, bar, parking.

Tongariro National Park

THC Chateau Tongariro. A Tourist Hotel Corporation hotel on the slopes of Mount Ruapehu; phone 899 Ruapehu. 84 rooms, all facilities, heated, restaurant, bars.

Wairakei

THC Wairakei Hotel. 48–021 Taupo. 75 rooms, restaurant, bar, thermal swimming pool, golf.

Waitomo Caves

THC Waitomo Hotel. Phone 948 Te Kuiti. Run by the Tourist Hotel Corporation, an oldish but redecorated hotel featuring solid comfort and good meals, 26 rooms with facilities, 17 without, restaurant, cocktail bar.

Waitomo Country Lodge. 17 rooms, restaurant, cocktail bar.

Wanganui

Bryvern Motor Inn. 321 Victoria Ave.; (064) 58–408. Restaurant, bars, parking.

Grand International Hotel. 99 Guyton St.; (064) 50–955. Restaurant, bars.

Wanganui Motel. 14 Alma Rd.; (064) 54–742. Restaurant, bar, pool.

Wellington

Bay Plaza Hotel. 40 Oriental Parade; (04) 857–799. 78 rooms, restaurant, bar.

Burma Motor Lodge. Burma Rd., Johnsonville, 8 miles from city; (04) 784–909. 63 rooms, restaurant, bar, parking.

City Life Apartments. 202 The Terrace; (04) 723–413. 50 quality, furnished apartments with daily maid service and full kitchen. Close to city center.

Host Harvey Hotel. Kemp St., Kilbirnie; (04) 872–189. 122 rooms, restaurant, bar, parking, 4 miles from city, 1 mile from airport.

Hotel St. George. Willis St.; (04) 739–139. 88 rooms, restaurant, bars, central.

Michael Fowler Hotel. Cable St.; (04) 852–809. 36 rooms, restaurants, bars, parking. Centrally located and exclusive.

Parkroyal Hotel. 360 Oriental Bay; (04) 859–949. 70 rooms, high quality, restaurants, bars, parking.

Plaza International. 148–176 Wakefield St.; (04) 733–900. 200 rooms, restaurants, bars, parking.

Plimmer Towers Hotel. Plimmers Lane, Lambton Quay, (04) 733–750. 100 rooms, upmarket, bars, restaurants, parking.

Port Nicolson Hotel. Corner Wakefield and Cambridge Terrace; (04) 845–903. 30 rooms, restaurant, bars, no parking.

Quality Inn. 100 Oriental Parade; (04) 850–279. 122 rooms, restaurant, bar.

Sharella Motor Inn. 20 Glenmore St.; (04) 723–823. 66 rooms, restaurant, bar, parking, ½ mile from city.

Terrace Regency. 345 The Terrace; (04) 859–829. High quality, 122 rooms suites, pool, bars, restaurant, parking.

THC James Cook Hotel. The Terrace; (04) 725–865. 270 rooms, restaurant, bars, parking.

West Plaza Hotel. 110–116 Wakefield St.; (04) 731–440. 102 rooms, restaurant, bar, central.

Home hospitality can be arranged by **Cottage Meals & Tours.** Don and Margaret Hoare, (04) 889–124, organize meetings and dining with New Zealanders in their homes and also home-stay stopovers. Sample charges: Bed and breakfast $56; dinner, bed, and breakfast $70; home-cooked dinner $38 (all based on 2 persons). Tour with car and driver, $22 per hr.

RESTAURANTS. Over the past few years, restaurants serving interesting and sophisticated cuisine have flourished. Good food is not hard to find, for New Zealand has an abundance of excellent and relatively inexpensive raw materials. Steak, lamb, and seafood are world-renown. New Zealand wine, like American, is variable in quality, but some reds and a great many white wines are well worth trying.

All the major hotels contain restaurants, and the larger cities, especially Auckland and Wellington, contain smaller establishments that serve attractive meals. You may pay anything from $30 to $50 per person for a three-course meal, but the cost is usually determined by the quality of the food rather than the reputation of the chef, or current fashion in dining. The most elegant restaurants can be more expensive.

By New Zealand law, restaurant staff are paid a living wage and do not depend upon tips for their livelihood. It is not necessary, then, to leave a tip, but your kindness will be appreciated if you do.

There are a number of smaller restaurants of the diner variety where a meal of steak and French fries can be had for as little as $8. In these, however, you cannot obtain alcoholic beverages. Many more expensive restaurants also lack a liquor license, but some will allow you to bring in your own wine.

Auckland

Antoine's. 333 Parnell Rd.; 798–756. Traditional French colonial atmosphere, French cuisine.

Carthews. 151 Ponsonby Rd.; 766–056. American cuisine, creole cooking.

Clichy Restaurant. 3 Britomart Pl.; 31–744. French provincial atmosphere, all French cuisine.

Da Gino. 66–68 Pitt St.; 770–973. Appropriate Italian decor and exclusively Italian food.

Fisherman's Wharf. Northcote Point; 483–955. Harborside nautical atmosphere, predominantly seafood menu.

Gamekeeper's. 29 Ponsonby Rd.; 789–052. Hunting lodge decor, game and local foods.

Le Gourmet. 1 Williamson Ave., Ponsonby; 769–499. Late-Victorian decor, limited specialized menu.

Harleys. 25 Anzac Ave.; 735–801. New Zealand food, with embellishments. BYO.

Hoffman's. 70 Jervois Rd., Herne Bay; 762–049. Award-winning restaurant with cocktail lounge and open fireplaces. Closed weekends.

Number Five. 5 City Rd.; 770–909. Top quality, superlative French nouvelle cuisine.

Oblio's. 110 Ponsonby Rd., Ponsonby; 763–041. An "indoor garden" restaurant, tasteful decor, and good food.

Orient. Strand Arcade, Queen St.; 797–793. Elegant Chinese decor with Chinese cuisine.

Orsini's. 50 Ponsonby Rd.; 764–563. Fine food in elegant surroundings.

Papillon. 170 Jervois Rd., Herne Bay; 765–367. Well-prepared and beautifully presented food; courtyard for pleasant summer dining. BYO.

Sardi's Restaurant & Piano Bar. Queens Arcades; 790–876. Good food in ultra smart surroundings.

Sails. Westhaven Marina; 789–890. A leading seafood restaurant with views of yachts.

Union Fish Company. 16 Quay St.; 796–745. Old renovated warehouse, unpreposing exterior but seafood is tops.

Yamato. 183 Karangahape Rd.; 771–424. Traditional Japanese food.

Bay of Islands (Paihia)

Most of the restaurants in this prolific fishing area specialize in seafood.
Bella Vista. Marsden Road; 27–451.
La Scala. Selwyn Road; 27–031.
The Tides. Williams Road; 27–557.

Napier

Beaches Restaurant. Marine Parade; 56–120. Seafood.
Dijon. Emerson St.; 53–976. European specialties.
Ormilie Lodge. Taradale; 445–774. European food.
Pickwick's Restaurant. Marine Parade; 56–120. Top-quality menu featuring New Zealand food.

New Plymouth

L'Escargot. 37 Brougham St.; 84–812. French provincial, small and compact.
Gareths. 182 Devon St. E.; 85–104. French and European food.
Juliana's. 393 Devon St. E.; 88–044. Flambé a specialty.
Ratanui Colonial Restaurant. 498 Carrington Rd.; 34–415. Old homestead out of town; graceful dining with fine silverware.

Rotorua

Aorangi Peak. Mountain Rd.; 86–957. 7 miles from the city, magnificent views, good food.

Caesars. Arawa St.; 70–984. Modern decor, international menu, licensed.

Colonel's Retreat. Little Village, Tyon St., Whakarewarewa; 81–519. International menu, jazz some nights.

Gazebo. Pukuatua St; 81–911. Continental cuisine.

Hoo Wah. 85–025. Chinese food, dine and dance Saturday.

Landmark. 1 Meade St.; 89–376. Early colonial decor, elegant; top New Zealand food.

Lewishams. 115 Tutanekai St.; 81–786. Tastefully quiet, good service, good food.

Poppy's. 4 Marguerita St.; 71–700. Restored historic villa, Edwardian decor, top-quality food.

Rumours. Pukuatua St.; 477–277. Continental-nouvelle cuisine, modern decor, BYO.

Suaves Restaurant & Cocktail Bar. Memorial Dr.; 82–001. Lakefront, cocktail and piano bar.

Tudor Towers. Government Gardens; 81–285. Cabaret and dancing.

You & Me. 31 Pukuatua St.; 476–178. French nouvelle cuisine, tasteful decor, delicious food.

Taupo

Downstairs. 703 Acacia Bay Rd.; 88–886. Dine and dance.
Echo Cliff. Corner Lake Terrace & Tongariro St.; 88–539. European cuisine.
Hilltop House. Ngamoutu Rd.; 89–015. Nouvelle cuisine.
Truffles. 116 Lake Terrace; 87–856. Lamb and game.

Tauranga

Charthouse Restaurant. Sulphur Point Marina; 83–001. Seafood a specialty.
Historic Restaurant. 17th Ave. W.; 83–337. Historic decor, European food.
Oliver's Restaurant. 111 Devonport Rd.; 86–704. Seafood and international cuisine.
La Salle. 59 The Strand; 89–349. French cuisine.

Wanganui

Bonne Maison. 321 Victoria Ave.; 58–408. French classical and nouvelle in turn-of-the-century surroundings.
Golden Oaks. 112 Liverpool St.; 58–309. European and New Zealand food.
Joseph's Restaurant. 13 Victoria Ave.; 55–825. Traditional New-Zealand food.

Wellington

Akiyoshi. 103 Willis St.; 731–189. Japanese food.
Bacchus Restaurant. 8 Courtenay Pl.; 846–592. Quiet, intimate, wide range of dishes.
Beefeater's Arms. 105 The Terrace; 738–195. Tudor decor, popular for business lunches. Specialty is rib of beef on the bone.
Il Casino and Il Salone. 108 Tory St.; 857–496. Good traditional Italian cuisine.
Genghis Khan Mongolian Restaurant. 25–27 Majoribanks St.; 843–592. Mongolian style barbecue fare set in a pleasant decor.
Grain of Salt. 232 Oriental Parade; 848–642. Contemporary decor, French cuisine with excellent harbor views.
Nicholson's. Rotunda Pavilion, 245 Oriental Parade; 843–835. European cuisine, set on the harbor waterfront with excellent views, contemporary decor.
Le Normandie. 116 Cuba St.; 845–000. Elegant old-fashioned decor, New Zealand game a specialty.
Orsini's. 201 Cuba St.; 845–476. Elegant, open fires in winter, quiet dining; seafood and steak.
Otto's Hafen Restaurant. Overseas Passenger Terminal; 845–436. Harbor views, specializes in fresh seafood.
Pierre's Restaurant. 342 Tinakori Rd.; 726–238. Early settler decor, small, intimate, French cuisine, no liquor license so bring your own wine.
Plimmer House. 99 Boulcott St.; 721–872. Gracious dining, Victorian decor, specialties are beef and seafood. Reservations.
The Roxburgh. 18 Majoribanks St.; 857–577. Small, intimate, international fare, German emphasis; open fire in winter.
Shorebird. 301 Evans Bay Parade; 862–017. Fresh fish caught from restaurant's own boat.
The Terrace Coachman. 97 The Terrace (entrance on Woodward St.); 738–170. Good food, quiet atmosphere. Specialties are duckling, scallops, and crayfish.
Varant Restaurant. 111 Pembroke Rd., Wilton; 785–324. In a suburb. Good French cuisine, BYO.
Yangtze Restaurant. Corner Jervois Quay and Williston St.; 728–002. Cantonese cuisine.

GETTING AROUND. Most towns are small and can be seen on foot. To get to attractions outside the cities, visitors should rent cars, join tours, or use local taxi companies.

Auckland

At the airport. Auckland's international airport (15 miles from the city) is adjacent to the domestic terminal so that transfers are common to both. An *Airporter* bus operates half-hourly services from the city and airport seven days a week, and taxis are available outside the terminals. The current fares are $6 by Airporter bus and $25 by taxi. The Airporter will also pick up passengers from certain hotels; call 275–0789.

By taxi. The two main taxi companies are: *Alert Taxis* (32–899) and *Auckland Co-Op Taxi Society* (792–792).

By rental car. The main Auckland firms are *Hertz*—in the U.S., 800–654–3131; in Auckland, 154 Victoria St. W., 34–924; *Avis*—in the U.S., 800–331–2112; in Auckland, 22 Wakefield St., 792–545; *Budget*—in the U.S., 800–527–0700; in Auckland, 26 Nelson St., 734–949.

Bay of Islands
(Paihia)

Paihia Taxis (27–506).

New Plymouth

New Plymouth Taxis (75–665).

Rotorua

Rotorua Taxi Federation (85–069).

Wanganui

Wanganui Taxis (54–444).

TOURS. Auckland. Auckland Visitors Bureau, 299 Queen Street (31–889), one block from the Civic Theater, has advice on a wide range of sightseeing options. Morning and afternoon coach tours are operated by the *Gray Line* (778–389) and *Scenic Tours* (640–189), visiting city sights, Mount Eden, Domain Park and gardens, Museum, Parnell Village, waterfront drive, harbor bridge, Kelly Tarlton's Underwater World. Pickups from major hotels can be arranged; otherwise departures from Downtown Airline Terminal. $28.

Napier. *Cox World Travel* runs a morning tour of Napier, Hastings, and Havelock North from 9:30 A.M. to 12:30 P.M. on Mon., Wed., and Fri., and an afternoon tour from 2 P.M. to 5:45 P.M. for sightseeing and visiting 8 major wineries. Call 58–574.

New Plymouth. Half- and full-day tours are run by *Newman's Sightseeing,* 23A Devon Mall (84–622) and *Pioneer Tours* (86–086).

Rotorua. *New Zealand Travel Office,* Fenton St. (85–179), and *Rotorua Promotions,* Hinemoa St. (84–066), will provide information. Almost all Rotorua's attractions can be reached by private automobile, but several companies operate regular sightseeing tours. Reservations may be made with the New Zealand Travel Office and often at hotels and motels or with individual operators. Most are half-day trips. N.Z. *Road Services,* Travel Center, Amohau St., next to the railway station, 81–039, extension 374. Tour 1: (Rotorua Grand Tour), 4 hours, visits Rotorua city sights, Agrodome, Rainbow Springs, Whakarewarewa, Maori Arts & Crafts Institute; $33. Tour 2: Herb Gardens and Whakarewarewa, 4 hours; $28. Tour 3: Skyline Rides and Whakarewarewa, 4 hours; $28. Tour 4: Waimangu Thermal Valley, Waiotapu, and Lady Knox Geyser, 5 hours; $29. Tour 5 (full-day tour): Waiotapu, Lady Knox Geyser, Waimangu Thermal Valley, the Te Wairoa Buried Village; $45. Tour 6: Te Wairoa Buried Village, 3 hours; $21. Tour 7: Agrodome and city highlights, 3 hours; $21. Tour 8: Agrodome and Fleur Orchid House, 3 hours; $27. Tour 9: city highlights, 2 ½ hours; $21. Tour 10: Skyline Rides and city highlights, 2 ½ hours; $21. Tours 1 to 4 are morning tours departing at 8:45 or 9 A.M. and Tours

6 to 10 are afternoon tours, departing from the travel center at 1:45 P.M. and the New Zealand Travel Office at 2 P.M.

Grayline Tours, Amohau St., 80–594, have morning and afternoon tours visiting Whakarewarewa, Rainbow Springs, Ohinemutum Kuirau Gardens, and Government Gardens, 3 ½ hours; depart New Zealand Travel Office 8:45 A.M. and 1:45 P.M.; $33. Waimangu Thermal Valley and Lake Rotomahana are visited on morning and afternoon tours, departing 8:45 A.M. and 1:45 P.M.; $49.50. Agrodome, Rainbow Springs, and Government Gardens morning tour, 3 ½ hours, departs 8:45 A.M.; $34. Te Wairoa Buried Village and Hell's Gate afternoon tour, 3 ½ hours, departs 1:45 P.M.; $34. There's a Rainbow Springs, Agrodome, and Whakarewarewa morning tour, 4 ½ hours, departing 8:45 A.M.; $42.

Tarawera Mountain Sightseeing Tour: 89–333. Half-day tour by four-wheel-drive cruiser to the summit of Mount Tarawera for a close-up view of the massive crater, 4 hours, 9:15 A.M. and 2 P.M. from N.Z. Travel Office; $38.

Waimangu Thermal Valley: The valley, about 16 miles from Rotorua, may be visited as a half-day trip with a return by the same route, or may be extended to a full-day trip with launch cruises on Lake Rotomahana and Lake Tarawera and then by coach to the Te Wairoa Buried Village and the Blue and Green Lakes and back to Rotorua (a circular route). Visitors walk through the valley, but a minibus is available for the return trip. For both trips, coaches depart from the New Zealand Travel Office at 8:45 A.M. The half-day trip costs $34, and the full-day trip $49.50. Take a packed lunch on the full-day trip or arrange with the coach driver to have a packed lunch, $6, available on the launch.

Wellington. The best way to see Wellington is to take a half- or full-day tour. The Wellington City Council has half-day tours leaving the Public Relations Office (735–063) on Mercer Street (opposite the Town Hall) at 10 A.M. and 2 P.M. daily. *Hammonds Sightseeing Tours* (847–539) has morning (10 A.M.–12:30 P.M.) and afternoon (2–4:45 P.M.) tours; an afternoon tour to the Gold Coast (2–4:45 P.M.) on Saturdays; and a full-day tour to the Wairarapa (departing 9:30 A.M.) on Sundays. Buses depart from the New Zealand Travel Office on Mercer Street.

Capital Elite Tours have 2 ½-hour city sightseeing tours leaving from the Public Relations Office at 9:30 A.M. at 1 P.M.; $22.

Cottage Meals and Tours (Don and Margaret Hoare), 899–124, arrange introductions and dining with New Zealanders in their homes as well as stopovers. Sample charges: Bed and breakfast, $67; dinner, bed, and breakfast, $99; home-cooked dinner, $38 (all based on two persons). Tour with car and driver, $40 per hour.

SPECIAL-INTEREST SIGHTSEEING. Auckland. There are a number of **harbor cruises,** which give excellent views of the city's skyline, ranging from the regular 45-minute ferry trips across to Devonport, to more extensive cruises by launch, catamaran, and yacht. *Pride of Auckland Cruises,* 734–557, operates a large sailing catamaran accommodating 60 people for two-hour cruises. Depart Quayside Launch Landing, Quay St., 9:30 A.M.–11:30 A.M., coffee cruise, $26; lunch cruise 12:30–2:30 P.M., $26 plus $11 lunch; afternoon coffee cruise 3–5 P.M., $26; dinner cruise 6–9 P.M., $56 including meal. 2 ½-hour cruises aboard its 50-ft "Challenger" depart 9:30 A.M. and 3 P.M. ($35); seafood lunch cruise ($40); dinner cruise ($66).

Fullers Captain Cook Cruises, Quay St., 394–901, offer large launch harbor cruises. Morning tea cruise 9:45–11:30 A.M., $21; volcanic island cruise 9:45 A.M.–2:30 P.M., $56; lunch cruise noon–2:15 P.M., $30; afternoon tea cruise 2:30–4 P.M., $21.

Scenic flights are offered by *Captain Al's Fantasy Flights,* Ardmore Airfield, 299–6456. Half-hour flights over city and outlying areas. Courtesy coach will pick up groups from hotels or motels, $89.

Of interest to women are Julie Steele's half-day Fashion Tours of shops and factories (397–442); $16, depart Downtown Airline Terminal.

The **Glenbrook Vintage Railway** (the term railroad is not used in New Zealand) is for railroad buffs and features a locomotive and railroad cars lovingly restored by enthusiasts. It is 58 kilometers south of Auckland city, and there is no organized transport. The train runs on several miles of track and the 40-minute ride operates from late October to June. Phone contact is 669–361.

Wine Tours. New Zealand wines are beginning to build a reputation, and a number of vineyards are within 30 kilometers of Auckland. Wine tours which visit the vineyards for free wine tasting, lunch, and cheeseboards are operated by A.G.M. Promotions (398–670) from 10 A.M. to 3 P.M. Mon. through Sat., with pick-ups from hotels/motels. Reservations are essential. Six vineyards are visited on each tour, but vary from day to day.

Napier. An interesting sidelight is a visit to a **sheepskin factory** *(Classic Decor Limited,* Thames Street, Pandora; phone 59–570) where you can see sheepskins going through the entire process of washing, cleaning, and shaping and finally made into floor rugs, car seat covers, soft toys and moccasins. Tours are at 11 A.M. and 2 P.M. Mon. through Fri. Your own transport is needed, though a taxi transport would not be expensive. Further information from the *Napier Public Relations Office,* Marine Parade (57–182).

Northland. No visit to Paihia or Russell would be complete without a **cruise,** either a half-day or a full-day, in the huge area enclosed by dozens of appealing and unspoiled islands and jutting headlands with inviting bays and beaches. A fast and exciting cruise is in one of the large diesel-powered catamarans operated by *Fullers Captain Cook Cruises,* which have cruising speeds of 20 knots and cover about 40 nautical miles. Air-conditioned suspension ensures a smooth ride in most conditions. The main cruise is to Cape Brett and Piercy Island and if weather permits a passage through the famous Hole in the Rock, a narrow tunnel where the promentary meets the sea, and a gentle entry into the Cathedral sea cave.

The bar serves spirits, beef, soft drinks and tea or coffee, but lunch must be ordered or take a picnic lunch with you. The half-day cruises depart Paihia at 10 A.M. and 12:30 P.M. daily, $37.

A similar but more leisurely cruise is by Fullers "Cream Trip" on a large launch seating 170 people with wide windows and comfortable seating. The launch delivers mail and supplies to outlying islands, $37. At Otehei Bay there is underwater marine life viewing by a submarine, $10. The launch has a bar and hostess service. The cruise leaves Paihia at 10 A.M. and returns at 3:15 P.M. Contact *Fullers Captain Cook Cruises* beside the wharf (27–421).

Rotorua. *Skyline Rides,* just 5 kilometers from the city center, can easily be seen from the road. A 900-meter gondola lift with a vertical rise of 200 meters takes you up the slopes of Mount Ngongotaha for panoramic views and a restaurant and cafe. Descent can be by gondola or by a 1-kilometer-long luge ride on a type of cart which has steering and braking and follows a curving track. Call 70–027.

Lake Cruise departs from lakefront wharf, 479–852. Cruises to Mokoia Island in the center of the lake in the launch *Ngaroto.* Coffee cruise 10 A.M. to noon and 2 to 4 P.M., $20; lunch cruise 12:30 to 2 P.M., $28 including lunch; barbecue cruise 7 to 10 P.M., $28 including barbecue. *Lakeland Queen Paddle Wheeler* departs from lakefront wharf (86–634). Coffee cruise 10–11:30 A.M. and 2:30–4 P.M., $13; lunch cruise 12:15 P.M.–1:45 P.M., $20 including lunch; dinner cruise 9 P.M.–midnight, $35.50 including dinner.

Ahuwhenua Farm Tour, 32–632, Bryce Rd., 12 miles southwest of Rotorua. Developed by two proud Maori farmers, the Ahuwhenua property is a 180-acre dairy farm milking 150 cows. Tour of farm and milking. Lunch provided. Visits by bus organized. $22.

Aerial Sightseeing: Because of the varied nature of its scenery, the Rotorua region lends itself well to aerial sightseeing. From the airport, 12 min. from the city, *Rotorua's Volcanic Wunderflites* (56–079) operates several aerial tours taking in Taupo and its lake, the thermal area, White Island (a still-active volcanic island off the east coast), the lake areas, forests, and Mount Tarawera. Costs range from $40 for a 15-minute flight to $407 for the Grand Volcanic Presentation. *The Helicopter Line* operates similar flights from $30 but adds a White Island Spectacular, with an actual landing on the island and a close inspection of the crater; $350 per person. Flights in beautifully restored vintage planes (an 8-passenger DH89 Dragon Rapide and an open-cockpit Tiger Moth) are offered by *White Island Airways* (59–832); $55–$165. From the downtown lakefront, *Float-Plane Air Services* operate sightseeing flights from $69 for 30 minutes to $330 for a landing on Matahina Hydro Lake and a jet-boat ride.

Wanganui. An offbeat side trip is a 2½-hour cruise up the river on the restored paddlewheel steamer *Otunui* (originally built in 1907) to Holly Lodge Estate Winery. The steamer leaves the City Marina at the end of Victoria Ave. (the main street) at 10 A.M. and returns at 12:30 P.M. Further information from Hospitality Wanganui (53–286).

Wellington. The *Kelburn Cable Car* (call 722–199) gives magnificent views of the city and harbor from the 480-foot summit at Kelburn. The entrance is on Cable Car Lane, almost opposite the T & G Building, off Lambton Quay. Cars run about every 10 minutes.

SPORTS. See also Facts at Your Fingertips for New Zealand and the introductory essay on fishing and hunting in New Zealand.

Boating. Contact *Charter Cruise Company,* Box 3730, Auckland, 734–557; *New Zealand Adventure Center,* Box 72–068, 399–192; or *South Seas Yacht Charter,* Box 38–366, Howick, Auckland; 534–2001.

Diving. Diving is a year-round sport in New Zealand, although it is most popular in summer. There are a variety of charters, but visitors may want to contact *Sportsways Aqua Lung Center,* 234 Orakei Rd. Remuera, Auckland; 542–117 or 546–268.

Golf. Visitors are welcome at the *Chamberlain Park Public Golf Course,* Linwood Ave., Mt. Albert, Auckland; 866–758.

Skiing and **river-rafting** packages are available through *Live-Life New Zealand Action Tours,* Box 4517, Auckland; 768–936. See Skiing, below.

Bay of Islands

Diving. Clear water in the Bay of Islands makes diving an exciting experience. Complete equipment and advice are available from *Paihia Dive & Charter,* Box 210, Paihia; 27–551.

Fishing. The Bay of Islands was made famous some years ago as a base for big game fishing by the author Zane Grey, who had his base at Otehei Bay on Urupukapuka Island. The most plentiful are striped marlin (which may weigh up to 150 kilograms), black marlin (often attaining more than 230 kilograms), and mako shark (over 100 kilograms). Best months are from Jan. to May. Charter boats are available from $350 to $450 a day from *Game Fishing Charters,* Maritime Building, Paihia; 27–311.

Rotorua and Taupo

Rotorua is one of New Zealand's most famous **trout fishing** areas, where fish average 4 lb. and often go up to 10 lb. Fly fishing requires skill, but you don't need any experience to catch a trout on Lake Rotorua, Lake Tarawera, or Lake Okataina. All you have to do is to drag a line with a lure behind a launch until a trout abandons caution and takes it. After that it's up to you to play it in carefully. If you are lucky, your hotel will probably cook and serve the fish for you. It's your only way of tasting trout as, being classified as a sporting fish, it cannot be sold commercially and therefore does not appear on hotel or restaurant menus.

There are a dozen or so fishing guides (members of the New Zealand Professional Fishing Guides Association) who offer trout-fishing excursions for rates averaging $50 an hour. Similarly, at Lake Taupo, advertisements appear in the local tourist newspaper, or contact the N.Z. Travel Office at Rotorua or the Public Relations Office at Taupo.

SKIING. Most fields have a ski season that extends from mid-June to early October. In addition to the commercial ski areas listed here, there are also ski clubs that welcome visitors. Contact the New Zealand Tourist and Publicity Dept. (see Facts at Your Fingertips) for further information.

Mt. Ruahepu in the center of the North Island boasts the most developed ski field in New Zealand, the *Chateau Ski Field,* with 2 double-chair lifts, three T-bars, and 3 pomas. Special areas for beginners. The ski field is 4½ hours from Auckland or Wellington. Accommodations available at Chateau Tongariro. For more information contact Chateau Tongariro, Tongariro National Park. Use a long-distance operator to call: MRP 809.

On the southwestern slopes of Mt. Ruahepu, 11 miles from the Ohakune township, lie the *Turoa Skifields.* The skifields offer 2 triple-chair lifts, 1 T-bar, 1 beginner's lift. For information phone 225 from Ohakune; 775–406 from Auckland. The information center is at 12 Clyde St., Ohakune.

HOT SPRINGS. In **Rotorua,** visitors to the *Polynesian Pools* in the Government Gardens can enjoy the mineral waters for as long they like. Some pools are open air, some enclosed, some private. Call 81–328.

THEME PARKS/HISTORIC SITES. *Heritage Park* is some 12 kilometers from Auckland at 3 Harrison Rd. (off the Ellerslie/Panmure Highway at Mount Wellington). A comparatively new development with a strong Maori influence, it is a theme park displaying agriculture, flora, fauna, and culture. Open daily from 9:30 A.M. to 5:30 P.M. Phone 590–424.

The *Tauranga Historic Village,* corner of Cameron Rd. and 17th Ave., Tauranga, is typical of early New Zealand townships and has period shops, cobblestone streets, and wares of a bygone age. Vintage transport is on display and there are rides on a train, a double-decker bus, or a horse and cart. Included is a gold-mining village, a Maori village, a military barracks and pioneering machinery. Hours are from 9 A.M. to 4 P.M. Phone 81–302.

ZOOS AND AQUARIUMS. *Auckland Zoological Park,* Motiono Rd., Western Springs, Auckland, is 5 minutes from downtown. The park contains a collection of exotic and native species and has a kiwi house. Open 9:30 A.M.–5:30 P.M. Small admission charge. Phone 761–415.

Kelly Tarlton's Underwater World is a bus ride from Auckland on Tamaki Drive, near Orakei Wharf. A 40-foot-long tunnel lined with large windows gives visitors a close-up view of sharks and stingrays—over 30 species of fish in all. Phone 580–603. Open 9 A.M. to 9 P.M., small admission charge.

MAORI HERITAGE. The *Maori Arts and Crafts Institute,* on Rotorua's southern edge near the entrance to the Whaka Reserve, preserves ancient Maori skills among young people. Visitors are welcome and there is a shop attached. Open 8 A.M.–5 P.M.; the carving school is closed on weekends and school holidays. Phone 89–047.

Ohaki Maori Village, near Waitomo Caves in Te Kuiti, is a model village where visitors can learn about pre-European Maori life. For information call 86–610.

One of the most enjoyable experiences in Rotorua is to attend a *Maori concert* and if possible to sample food cooked in the Maori way in an earth oven (a *hangi*). The traditional Maori way is to heat stones in a pit, into which the food—meat, fish, and vegetables—is placed in woven flax baskets. The pit is then covered and the food left to steam. In Rotorua, however, natural super-heated underground steam is used in many cases, which saves a great deal of time, though the principle is the same. You can enjoy a Maori concert and/or *hangi* at the following: *Rotorua Maori Cultural Theater,* 85–912 or 86–591, 7 P.M. daily, $7, bookings not required. *Tamatekapua Meeting House,* Ohinemutu Village, 8 P.M. daily, $9, no bookings required.

Maori Arts & Crafts Institute, (see above), concerts 12:15 P.M. daily from mid-Oct. to the end of Mar.; thereafter May and Aug. school holidays only; $6. *Maori Hangi and Concerts* (reservations essential). *THC International Hotel,* corner Froude and Tyron sts., Whakarewarewa, 81–189, 6:30 P.M. daily, $28. *TraveLodge,* Eruera St., 81–174, 7 P.M. daily, $28. *Tudor Towers,* Government Gardens, 81–285, 7 P.M. daily, $24. *Geyserland Resort,* Fenton St., Whakarewarewa, 82–039, 6 P.M. daily, $26. *Sheraton Hotel,* Sala St., 87–139, 7 P.M. daily, $30. *Hyatt Kingsgate,* Hinemaru St., 477–677. Polynesian festival, 7:30 P.M. daily: $39.

See also Museums and Galleries, below and Special-Interest Sightseeing and Tours, above.

MUSEUMS AND GALLERIES. There is more to New Zealand than spectacular scenery, and rainy days can become a perfect time to learn more about the country's art and artifacts.

Auckland

Auckland City Art Gallery. Wellesley and Kitchener sts.; 792–020 or 069. One of the finest public art collections in New Zealand, the holdings at the gallery include European art, contemporary international prints, and New Zealand art past and present. Mon.–Thurs., 10 A.M.–4:30 P.M.; Fri. to 8:30 P.M.; Sat. and Sun. 1–5:30 P.M. Free.

Microworld of Inner Space. Corner Halsey and Madden sts. (393–256). This unique museum has 90 visitor-operated "micro-scanners," which magnify subjects up to 500 times and penetrate the inner life of rocks, food, fabrics, dentistry, the blood stream, forensic science, among other things. Open daily 9 A.M.–11 P.M.; $7.50.

Museum of Transport and Technology. A few miles from city center, in great North Rd., Western Springs; 860–198. A fascinating collection of methods of transportation, among other items. Accessible by city bus. Open daily, except Christmas, 9 A.M.–5 P.M. Admission charge.

War Memorial Museum. In the Auckland Domain; 30–443. Noted for its outstanding collection of Maori art, the museum is also a memorial to the dead of the two world wars. Displays also feature New Zealand's natural history. Open daily 10 A.M.–5 P.M., from 11 A.M. Sun. Accessible by Auckland bus.

Gisborne

Gisborne Museum and Arts Centre, 18–22 Stout St. (83–832), features Maori works as well as natural exhibits. Local artists and craftspeople also display their works here. 10 A.M.–4:30 P.M., Tues.–Fri.; from 2 P.M. on Sat., Sun., holidays. Small admission charge.

Hamilton

Hamilton Arts Center, corner of Victoria and Marlborough sts. (390–685), features changing exhibits of contemporary art.

Waikato Museum of Art and History, 150 London St. (392–118), displays art as well as Maori and European history exhibits. Tues.–Sat., 10 A.M.–4:30 P.M.; from noon, Sun. and holidays. Admission is free.

New Plymouth

Govett-Brewster Art Gallery (85–149) is considered by many to be one of the most exciting art galleries in the country.

Taranaki Museum (89–583) displays a fine collection of Maori artifacts.

Rotorua

Rotorua Art Gallery and **City of Rotorua Museum** (86–382) are inside Tudor Towers within the Government Gardens. The art gallery displays works of native New Zealand and international artists. Small admission to each.

Wanganui

Wanganui Regional Museum is in the Civic Center, at the end of Maria Place. The largest regional museum in New Zealand; here is displayed a large Maori collection and historical exhibits. Open weekdays 9:30 A.M.–4:30 P.M.; weekends 1–5 P.M. Small admission charge. Call 57–443.

Wellington

Alexander Turnbull Library, 44 the Terrace, houses records from early New Zealand: books, pamphlets, newspapers, manuscripts, prints, paintings, photographs. 9 A.M.–5 P.M.; to noon Sat. Call 722–107.

Artours, 727–018, run by the New Zealand Crafts Council, are guided tours to arts and crafts galleries and studios; from 9 A.M. to 5 P.M. Mon. to Sat., groups 4 to 6, $85 and $60 per person.

The National Art Gallery (phone 859–703) and **National Museum** (859–609) are on Buckle St. The art gallery features paintings by New Zealanders, but also has a large collection of European works. The museum displays exhibits of South Pacific, New Zealand, and Maori history. 10 A.M.–4:45 P.M. daily. Accessible by bus from Wellington if you're willing to walk a little. Admission is free at both.

Southward Vintage Car Museum. Vintage car buffs should certainly not miss this. Situated two miles north of Paraparamumu (37 miles from Wellington) on Otaihanga Road, the museum has one of the largest and most comprehensive collections of vintage automobiles in the southern hemisphere. The collection comprises some 250 vehicles, more than half of which are on show at any one time. There is, for instance, a 1915 Indianapolis Stutz, a 1907 Holsman, a 1904 Wolseley, a 1913 Maudslay, and a 57C Bugatti, and even one of gangster Al Capone's cars with bullet holes in the glass.

ARTS AND ENTERTAINMENT. In **Auckland,** visitors can enjoy the range of theatrical productions offered by the *Mercury Theater,* 9 France St., 33–869, and *Theater Corporate,* 14 Galatos St., 774–307. Watch the local papers for other cultural events, such as performances by *The Symphonia.*

A variety of theater experiences are offered by the *Downstage Theater* in **Wellington.** In the Hannah Playhouse on Cambridge Terr. (849–639), the group is very popular and tickets should be reserved well in advance.

THE SOUTH ISLAND

"The Mainland"

The starting point of a journey through the extraordinary scenery of the South Island is usually Christchurch, which is reached by air from just about everywhere in New Zealand. It is a good point of arrival, as it typifies the different characteristics of the two islands. While Christchurch is a busy commercial city, it is more gracious than those in the North Island and the pace of life seems more relaxed. Its intensive civic pride is exemplified by numerous city gardens and parks and by the lovely gardens of private homes.

The South Island is larger than the North, and the South Island people like to refer to it as the Mainland.

To the south, the main highlights are Mount Cook, Queenstown, Lake Te Anau, Lake Manapouri, and Milford Sound. All can be reached by good roads, but almost a full day is required between each point, and most visitors use the regular services of Ansett New Zealand, with its turbo-jet planes. The pilots add enjoyment by giving detailed commentaries as points of special interest are passed.

On a time-restricted itinerary it is possible to fly to Mount Cook, take a ski-plane flight with a landing on the glacier, and be back in Christchurch that night, having included a glimpse of Queenstown. Changing planes at Queenstown one can even fly into Milford Sound. As this is alpine country, all depends on favorable weather. But having come this far in the South Pacific, one should make the most of it and allow a week or more, to enjoy some outstanding scenic spectacles and sightseeing experiences.

As the plane leaves Christchurch the vast checkerboard of green and brown cultivated fields of the Canterbury Plains unfolds, and soon the plane is flying along the chain of permanently snow-clad summits of the Southern Alps. As far as the eye can see there is a jumbled mass of rugged peaks.

In a little over half an hour the plane crosses the divide at about 7,500 ft. and, as it does so, the majesty of Mount Cook and the sister mountains clustering around her are suddenly revealed. Below is the 18-mile-long Tasman Glacier, down which the plane flies. Sheer icy cliffs rise beside and above you as the plane gradually loses height to land at the airport, which has an altitude of 2,500 ft. The clarity of the air makes the mountains seem almost at the wing tip; in fact they are a mile or more away.

From the Mount Cook airport the plane flies down the length of the Tasman River and over the green-blue glacial Lake Pukaki and swings to the right. On the left is the alpine plateau of the Mackenzie Country, named after a Scottish sheep stealer who found a pass to it through the mountains; to the right is lovely Lake Ohau. Soon the blue waters of Lake Wakatipu and tree-studded Queenstown come into view, and the plane sweeps over the deep valleys, silver rivers and fertile farms to land.

From here, smaller planes fly the exciting scenic round-trip flight to Milford Sound, where one can stop overnight, and return next day by road. Alternatively, continue to Te Anau, and make that a base for a trip to the sound by road.

That is the aerial tour for the visitor in a hurry, but some of New Zealand's most enchanting travel experiences will be missed. Mount Cook demands a day to absorb the grandeur of the surrounding mountains, and savor the ski-plane flight to the full. As one visitor put it, "Queenstown is good for the soul." An unhurried sampling of the wealth of beautiful and unusual sidetrips amply repays a visit of three days.

Milford Sound cannot be appreciated in all its majestic glory and grandeur on a flying visit for, unless a half-day is allowed for a launch cruise down the sound, a truly moving experience is missed.

Lakes Te Anau and Manapouri offer their own unique attractions. Each has its individual charm: Manapouri for its somber beauty and Te Anau for its glowworm cave. The road from Te Anau to Milford Sound must rank as one of the most spectacular scenic drives in New Zealand.

The Fertile Southland

Farther to the south are Southland, so fertile that farmers can run up to eight sheep to the acre, and Invercargill, the southernmost city, famous for its succulent oysters. To the east is Dunedin, founded by the Scottish immigrants, and proud of its title as the Edinburgh of the South.

If you look at a relief map of the South Island you will see quite clearly how the Southern Alps form a backbone for much of the length of the island. Only three passes give access to the west coast. Consequently, this delightful region is too seldom visited, for it is a place of magnificent seascapes, tranquil alpine lakes, verdant subtropical forest, and the Franz Josef and Fox glaciers.

From Christchurch the West Coast can be reached through the Lewis Pass and Arthur's Pass, both distinguished for natural beauty, and from Queenstown through the Haast Pass, spectacular in an entirely different way. A popular route, especially for organized tours, is from Christchurch to the glaciers, through the Haast Pass to Lake Wanaka and Queenstown, Lake Te Anau and Milford Sound, back to Queenstown, and then on to Mount Cook and back to Christchurch.

The northern part of the South Island above Christchurch, which is highly popular with New Zealanders, is often omitted by overseas visitors as it is apart from the main route. The Marlborough Sounds, a maze of sunken valleys, has hundreds of miles of inland waterways which afford excellent fishing. Nelson, a placid city, is the heart of a large fruit- and tobacco-growing area, with some of the most delightful beaches to be found anywhere and a climate that lures people into retirement there.

Although they have a common bond, the North and South islands are entirely different. The South Island undoubtedly has the greater number of scenic attractions.

CHRISTCHURCH

"Gracious" is a fitting term for Christchurch, the South Island's largest city. With a population of nearly 300,000, it is the hub of the extensive Canterbury district and the main point of arrival for travelers from the North Island and many from Australia.

Christchurch is often described as the garden city of New Zealand and richly deserves its title. Within its confines are about a thousand acres of parkland and gardens, and through the city itself meanders the small and restful Avon River, fringed with willows and bordered by sloping grassy banks. Householders take pride in their gardens, and competitions are held every year for the finest garden and best-kept street.

It has also been said of Christchurch that it is "more English than the English," and the most English city outside England. Certainly many aspects of it and many of its buildings are reminiscent of England, for it was planned that way.

It was settled under the auspices of the Church of England and was planned for English people belonging to the Anglican Church. In 1850 the "First Four Ships" brought a group of English settlers to the port of Lyttelton, and the Canterbury pilgrims made their historic trek over the steep Port Hills to the fertile plains beyond. The older Canterbury families proudly trace their lineage to these ships, just as Americans are proud to claim that their forebears came over on the *Mayflower.*

The settlers found their city already surveyed and laid out in broad regular streets, some named after Church of England bishoprics, such as Worcester, Hereford, and Gloucester. Canterbury's planners saw the colony as part of England transplanted to New Zealand.

Colonization went ahead rapidly. By 1865 all the available land on the Canterbury Plains had been cultivated and sheep farms carried more than a million sheep. In the 1880s the success of refrigerated shipping revolutionized farming in Canterbury. Small towns and villages, the centers of farming areas, grew up. An irrigation system solved the problem of watering stock, new areas were opened up by railroads, and the large holdings were divided to make land available for small farms. Today, Canterbury is New Zealand's chief wheat-growing district, as well as the home of world-famed Canterbury lamb.

Christchurch was planned and built around the beautiful Christchurch Cathedral. Like many of the city's early buildings, the cathedral is Gothic in design and built of rough gray local stone. The bells duplicate the upper ten of St. Paul's Cathedral, London. Gothic architecture, undergoing a revival when the first buildings of Christchurch were erected, was used for many of the early structures: schools, the museum, the old provincial-council chambers and Canterbury University College. There is a charm and stability about these early stone buildings, sheltered by English trees planted by the city's forefathers.

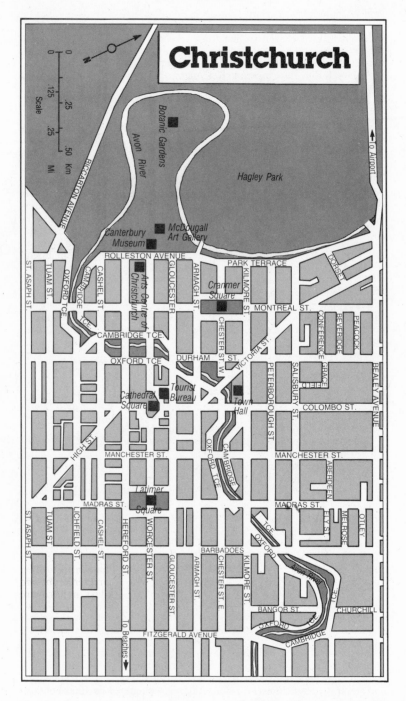

To the south of the city rise the Port Hills. From the 24-mile scenic Summit Road extending along their crests there are fine views of the Canterbury Plains and the Southern Alps and, to the east, the peaceful bays of Lyttelton Harbor and the hills of Banks Peninsula. The French established a colony on the peninsula in 1840. Had they done so a little earlier they could well have claimed New Zealand for France before the Treaty of Waitangi was signed, establishing British sovereignty over all New Zealand. The French attempt was abandoned nine years later.

Christchurch has long been a New Zealand base for exploration of the Antarctic. The British explorer Robert Falcon Scott, whose party of five reached the South Pole in 1912, left from here (his statue stands by the Avon River), and it is now the headquarters of Operation Deep Freeze. Nonstop 2,200-mile flights are made in summer, from the international airport to McMurdo, the main United States base in Antarctica. New Zealand exercises control over the Ross Dependency and maintains Scott Base, near McMurdo.

Scenic Tours

Afternoon bus tours are run by the Christchurch Transport Board. Easy two-hour morning and afternoon escorted walking tours of the city's main attractions, or escorted tours in your own vehicle, are available from Personal Guiding Services. Contact the NZTP Travel Office or Canterbury Information Center.

Christchurch Cathedral

The graceful Christchurch Cathedral dominates the heart of the city. The foundation stone was laid in 1864, just 14 years after the arrival of the first organized settlers sponsored by the Church of England. From the balconies to the bell chamber (133 steps up) there are magnificent views of the city and a glimpse of the Southern Alps on a clear day. Choral evensong is sung by the Cathedral Choir on Tuesdays and Wednesdays at 5:15 P.M.; and by the Boy Choristers on Fridays at 4:30 P.M. The tower is open from 9 A.M. to 4 P.M. weekdays and Saturdays and 1 P.M. to 4:30 P.M. on Sundays; admission 50 cents. The cathedral is open for prayer or a visit from 8 A.M. to 5 P.M.

Cathedral Square

Cathedral Square stands at the very heart of the city, and all the main streets radiate from it. Once a busy bus terminal, it has now been cleared of traffic and made into a delightfully decorated pedestrian area. A "speaker's corner," where those who have a cause to advocate can give their message, is popular at lunchtime.

The Christchurch Wizard has become a nationally known institution as an orator, entertainer, and fun maker. Dressed in a sorcerer's robe and a wide-brimmed coned hat, he performs at 1 P.M. on weekdays in the square and orates on subjects that interest him at the time. He is witty and provocative but never offensive. If he feels strongly enough he will impose a "curse." It is all good fun, and the Wizard obviously enjoys the performances as much as the crowd does.

Christchurch Town Hall

This is less an administrative building than a cultural complex containing a concert auditorium, a theater, a banquet room, and a restaurant. It was opened in 1972 and is one of the finest in the Southern Hemisphere. It incorporates the latest in theater and auditorium design, and its pleasing exterior is set off by a small lake and fountain.

Canterbury Museum

An entire Christchurch street after the style of the 1850s can be explored. Shop windows display their goods, cottages are fully furnished, and there is even an old fashioned horse cab. The ornithological section is particularly well designed, with birds displayed in realistic dioramas.

The Hall of Antarctic Discovery contains a well-displayed history of Antarctic exploration and a superb collection of equipment used by successive parties which have visited Antarctica. A graphic idea of the scientific knowledge that has resulted can be gained from static and moving diagrams, dioramas of penguins, seals, and whales, and sound recordings of them.

Botanical Gardens

In keeping with the garden-city reputation, the Botanical Gardens are a delight. A section is devoted entirely to New Zealand plants, and the rose, water, azalea, and rock gardens are outstanding. Tropical plants may be seen in the begonia house, and there is a splendid display of cacti in the succulent house.

McDougall Art Gallery

Just behind the museum is the McDougall Art Gallery, which contains classic paintings of the Maori by the noted artists Lindauer and Goldie.

Sign of the Takahe

Henry George Ell, who died in 1934, was a visionary. He planned a series of rest houses along the Summit Road of the Port Hills. He began three but only one, the Sign of the Takahe (a New Zealand bird), was completed. It takes the shape of an English baronial hall of the Tudor period. Made of stone quarried from the Port Hills and from native timbers, the building was fashioned by hand. Its fine carvings, coats of arms, heraldic shields and stained glass windows bring a touch of old-time England to these southern hills.

Ferrymead Historic Park and Transport Museum

Still in the process of development, this technological museum is a journey into the past. There are displays of old trolley cars and railroad locos and horse-drawn vehicles. The Hall of Wheels houses vintage autos and machinery and early 20th-century appliances.

Orana Wildlife Park

Animals from various parts of the world have been assembled in this 10-acre drive-through wildlife park, not far from the center of the city. Lions, tigers, camels, and others roam freely in a natural environment.

Willowbank Wildlife Reserve

This reserve contains probably the largest collection of birds and animals in the South Island and includes mountain lions, camels, donkeys, and deer. A farmyard section has Scottish highland cattle, primitive sheep and other ancient livestock breeds, as well as old farm implements and vehicles.

Mount Cook

This towering pinnacle of 12,349 ft. is New Zealand's highest mountain. The Maoris called it *Aorangi* (the Cloud Piercer). But it is now, of course, named after Captain Cook, who never actually saw it.

Mount Cook is in the very heart of New Zealand's most spectacular mountain region, almost in the center of the long chain of permanently snow-capped Southern Alps stretching down much of the South Island. Yet it does not stand alone—surrounding it are 17 peaks, all exceeding 10,000 ft.—and Mount Sefton, Mount Tasman, and Mount La Perouse are only a little lower.

Rising to what appears to be a sharp point (though there are three peaks on the summit ridge), Mount Cook is indeed a monarch among mountains, its steep slopes glistening with ice and snow. Those who first saw it thought that it would never be climbed. It was—but not until Christmas Day 1894. It has since been climbed many times, and by the first woman, Freda du Faur, in 1913. It was here that Sir Edmund Hillary, the first to conquer Mount Everest, did much of his early mountaineering.

Glaciers abound on the mountain slopes, including the 18-mile Tasman Glacier, one of the longest in the world. From the hotel, 2,500 ft. above sea level and well below the snow line, it is not uncommon to hear the dull roar of an avalanche high in the mountains, particularly on Mount Sefton.

Two natural inhabitants are of interest. The area is one of the homes of the kea, a New Zealand bird rather like a large parrot with deep green plumage and a vivid crimson breast. They are amusing birds, inquisitive and fearless, but beware of leaving anything bright or shiny about; it will quickly disappear or be pecked to pieces by their strong beaks. The name comes from the sound of their cry. Although they are not large, they have the reputation of being sheep killers. It is said that a flock will chase a sheep until it is exhausted and then alight on its back and dig with their cruel beaks for the kidneys.

Seldom seen except by hunters, thar and chamois also inhabit the mountains. Liberated in 1904, they found the environment similar to their native Himalayas, and thrived to such an extent that they have been declared noxious animals because of the damage they do to vegetation.

Growing profusely on the alpine slopes are the delicate white flowers of what are known as Mount Cook lilies. This is not, however, a true lily but a variety of *ranunculus lyallii.* It is used as the insignia of Mount Cook Airlines.

Arriving by road (or flying from Mount Cook to Queenstown) you pass through or over a large plateau of brown tussock and grass bounded by long ranges of hills. This is the Mackenzie Country, named after a Scottish sheep stealer. Mackenzie, who spoke only Gaelic, found a pass through the mountain barrier in the mid 1800s and would sneak with his dog down to farms in the lower levels, round up sheep, and drive them back to the plateau. Caught eventually, he was given a five-year jail sentence. He begged to be allowed to take his dog with him to prison but was refused. The dog was taken south, and her offspring were eagerly sought by shepherds. Mackenzie escaped three times in the first year and was finally released on condition that he leave the country and never return.

Good sheep dogs were indispensable to the early settlers in this remote and spartan area. At Lake Tekapo, at the edge of the Mackenzie Country and just off the main road from Christchurch on the way to Mount Cook, stands a bronze statue of a sheep dog, erected as a tribute.

Here too is the charming rural Church of the Good Shepherd, built of stone as a memorial to the pioneer sheep farmers of the region. The backdrop to the altar is a large window, filled with a magnificent panorama of the blue-green waters of the glacial lake and the mountains behind.

Ski-Plane Flights

A wonderful way to see the New Zealand scenery. Where else in the world can you take off at 2,500 ft. and within 20 minutes land at about 7,000 ft. on the vast snowfields at the head of a glacier? Many tourists go to Mount Cook as much for this flight as to see the mountain.

The aircraft has wheels for use at the Mount Cook airport, but it is also fitted with retractable skis. You take off from the airfield in front of the Hermitage Hotel, and within minutes you are flying amid peaks sheathed in perpetual ice, over snow valleys, and beside glittering icefalls. The slopes seem close enough to touch, but distances are deceptive in the clear mountain air, and they are actually at least a quarter of a mile away. Below you the rock-strewn surface of the Tasman Glacier gives way to pure ice, hundreds of feet deep, and then you are above the huge snowfields at the head of the glacier.

The skis are lowered, and the plane glides onto the snow and hisses to a stop. You get out into the soft snow—and find yourself in complete silence, in a place that once only mountaineers could reach. Armchair mountaineering if you like, or, as one visitor put it, instant Hillary. Only the most insensitive could fail to be emotionally stirred.

After a few minutes for photographs, the plane takes off again and you fly around Mount Cook, with a view of the two glaciers flowing down the opposite side into native forest and the Tasman Sea. Then down the Meuller Glacier and back to the airport. Known as the Grand Circle, the flight takes an hour, and no special clothing is needed.

The ingenuity of a New Zealander made this flight possible. The late Harry Wigley (later Sir Henry), head of Mount Cook Airlines and its coach-touring company, had flown light planes in this region before and after the war, during which he was a well-known pilot. He designed his retractable skis, had his company workshops make a prototype. On September 22, 1955, Wigley and one of his men made the first ski-plane landing. As he writes in his book *Ski Plane Adventure:*

"For several seconds not a word was said. We just sat and looked at each other. Then we slowly opened the doors and stepped out into the deep, soft, powder snow almost up to our knees. We felt like two blowflies sitting on the South Pole."

Now landing on the glacier is commonplace. Ski-plane flights are very popular and dependent on the weather, so it is wise to reserve as soon as possible after you arrive at the Hermitage or Glencoe Lodge or with the Mount Cook Line at the airport; phone 849. The cost is NZ$201.

Skiing and Mountain Climbing

Skiing and mountain climbing in the area are superb. Alpine Guides, at Mt. Cook Village, offer heli-skiing, glacier skiing, ski touring, cross-country skiing, and a school of mountaineering; phone 834.

National Park Headquarters

Here you can see collections of mountaineering equipment and exhibits of local flora and fauna and specimen rocks peculiar to the region.

Christchurch to Mount Cook by Road

Mount Cook is 211 miles (339.5km) from Christchurch by road—a good day's drive. For about 60 miles (96.5km) the road heads straight through the rich Canterbury Plains, which were formed by the wearing down of the high country by snow or glacier-fed rivers rising in the Southern Alps. Some of these are quite large, and all are swift-flowing and change their courses continuously—hindering the efforts of soil conservation authorities, who have tried to confine the waters to regular channels with protection works of willow and embankments. Anglers, however, are delighted, as the rivers are the haunt of brown trout and quinnat salmon. The Selwyn River is unusual in that it flows underground for much of the year.

The road then swings inland into the rolling lamb country of Canterbury and Fairlie, nearly a thousand feet above sea level, and in coaching days a staging place on the journey to Mount Cook. It then follows the pleasant Opihi Valley and climbs through Burke's Pass to 2,000 ft. The long chain of the Southern Alps is now clearly in view.

A gentle downhill grade brings you to Lake Tekapo, 15 miles long and 620 ft. deep, the site of a glacier that flowed in prehistoric times. 30 miles (42km) on is Lake Pukaki, 1,588 ft. above sea level. Both Lake Tekapo and Lake Pukaki are sites of extensive hydroelectric developments.

On the 36-mile (52km) run to Mount Cook the road follows the shore of Lake Pukaki for 15 miles and then heads up the mountain-flanked Tasman Valley to the Hermitage complex. In clear weather the views of the high alps are breathtakingly beautiful.

Mount Cook to Queenstown by Road

After following the Tasman River for 36 miles (52km) to Lake Pukaki, turn right and head south. For 26 miles the road crosses comparatively flat country, through which the Ohau River flows. The river drains Lake Ohau, another glacial lake and also a source of the Waitaki River.

After leaving the township of Omarama there is a fairly steep ascent to the 3,300-ft. summit of the Lindis Pass through hills covered with brown tussock and grass, then a descent through the Lindis Gorge. From ancient times a well-worn track used by the Maoris ran from Wanaka over the Lindis Pass and down the banks of the Waitaki River to the coast.

About 112 miles (180km) from the township of Tarras, there are two routes to Queenstown. To the right the road leads to Lake Wanaka and then climbs over the 3,676-ft. Crown Range, dropping down to Arrowtown and continuing to Queenstown. The more popular route, however, is straight on to Cromwell at the junction of the Clutha and Kawarau rivers. This was the scene of intense gold mining activities in the 1860s, and dredging is still carried on in the Clutha River.

The next 22 miles is through the winding Kawarau Gorge, with its many relics of the gold-mining days. Of special interest is the Roaring Meg Stream, which operates a tiny powerhouse. The remainder of the journey is through pleasant farm country. At the crest of a hill, pause to admire tree-ringed Lake Hayes, famed for its lovely reflections.

As the route is sparsely populated, but full of lovely picnicking spots, have the hotel pack you a box lunch.

Queenstown

Picturesque is a word too frequently used in tourist brochures; yet it is difficult to find a more appropriate adjective for Queenstown. It is a small, well-kept township of 3,000 permanent residents but thronged with visitors throughout the year. Most leave with regret that they have not allowed enough time to enjoy it more. Though reliant on tourism for its prosperity, it has avoided gross commercialism. The outstanding quality of the scenery and the variety of sightseeing make exploitation unnecessary.

Queenstown delights the mind as well as the eye. It stands on the middle shores of Lake Wakatipu, facing two imposing peaks and flanked by the saw-toothed 7,500-ft. range of the Remarkables. It is often difficult to believe one is not at an alpine lake in Switzerland.

Queenstown can be enjoyed in all four seasons. In winter it resounds to the laughter of young skiers, in spring the trees begin to show their greenery, in summer it is a place for swimming, sunbathing, and boating, and in the fall it is a blaze of color. The early settlers planted deciduous trees in this originally treeless area and, as fall arrives, the willows and poplars, elms and larches, sycamores and maples splash the brown landscape with a riot of color.

Lake Wakatipu, shaped like a giant letter S, is 52 miles long and varies from one to three miles in width. It is 1,016 ft. above sea level, and its greatest depth is 1,310 ft., which means that its floor is 294 ft. below sea level. It has been called the Lake That Breathes, as its waters rise and fall 3 inches every 15 minutes. The Maoris noticed this and created a legend. In revenge for carrying off his bride-to-be, an angered lover set fire to a giant as he lay sleeping in the fern. The pain of the fire caused the giant to draw up his knees, and so intense was the heat that he sank deep into the earth and burned until nothing remained but his ashes and his heart, which kept beating. The rains and rivers filled the chasm, but the outline of the lake retained his figure. The waters of the lake, says the legend, still pulsate to the beating of the giant's heart.

Hard-headed scientists, however, give a more prosaic explanation. The pulsations, they say, are caused by wind or variations in atmospheric pressure. A pity. The Maori legend is more colorful.

High in the affection of Queenstown residents, and much admired by visitors, is the T.S.S. *Earnslaw,* a steamer built in 1912 and still in service. Her gleaming white hull and red funnel capped with a black band blend harmoniously with the mountain and lake backdrops. The Lady of the Lake, they call her. Weighing 335 tons, she was prefabricated in Dunedin in 1912 and assembled at Kingston, at the southern end of the lake. Until a road was cut around the lake comparatively recently, she was the only means of servicing the lakeside farms, and she worked hard transporting not only stores but also sheep and cattle. If you have time, don't miss a half-day or full-day cruise up the lake. If you're mechanically minded, you'll enjoy peering down at the engine room with its gleaming, lovingly maintained machinery, watching the boilers being stoked with coal to drive the twin screws and smelling the pungent hot oil.

In spite of the then difficult access the first settlers established sheep farms, but in 1862 an event occurred which changed the history of the area. Gold, in plentiful supply, was found, and New Zealand's biggest gold rush began. The Shotover River was termed the richest river in the world. Thousands of miners converged from many parts of the world.

Gradually, the bounteous supplies dwindled, and the miners either settled or left. A little gold is still found, but the finest gold in Queenstown today is the burnished leaves on the trees in fall. Everywhere, however, are interesting relics of those days of gold fever—abandoned workings, crude stone cottages, culverts to carry water for washings, and the huge mounds of stone tailings from the dredges.

Exploring Queenstown

Queenstown has such a wide range of beautiful and unusual side trips that a week could be spent doing something new every day.

Lake Cruises

Several cruises are operated by the historic T.S.S. *Earnslaw.* A one-hour lunch cruise departs at 12:30 P.M. daily August to June; a longer cruise, giving views of the lake shores and the head of the lake and a visit to Mount Nicholas Sheep Station, departs at 2 P.M. August to June; and you can dine on board on an evening cruise departing at 7 P.M. December thru March. There are also faster, enclosed hydrofoil cruises. Book cruises through Fiordland Travel Services on the wharf on Beach St.

Also on the wharf is an underwater observatory where you climb down 15 feet below the water into a viewing lounge to see wild trout, quinnat salmon, longfin eels, and ducks living free in their own environment.

Skyline Chalet

From almost anywhere around Queenstown you'll see a chalet perched on Bob's Peak 1,530 ft. above the town. It is reached by an aerial cableway with small gondolas, and from the restaurant at the top there are spectacular panoramic views. Open 10 A.M. to 9 P.M.; small admission charge. *Kiwi Magic,* a 25-minute adventure program, is shown on the hour. Cost: NZ$7.

Queenstown Domain

Sometimes called the Government Gardens (they were developed by the government), the Queenstown Domain extends along a peninsula occupying one side of the bay and presents a colorful display of bright flower beds, lily ponds, exotic shrubs and trees, and a sports area. Near the tip is a large glacial boulder commemorating five Antarctic explorers.

Queenstown Motor Museum

Close to the base terminal of the cableway, this museum displays a very good collection of vintage cars—a 1903 De Dion, a 1909 Renault and a 1922 Rolls Royce Silver Ghost, to name a few. 9 A.M. to 5:30 P.M.

Kingston Flyer and Shotover Jet

These two outstanding Queenstown attractions are musts for every visitor. The Kingston Flyer is a 1920s steam passenger train that runs from Kingston, at the bottom of Lake Wakatipu, to Fairlight, a pretty farming community set in rolling hill country 15 miles away.

The Shotover Jet, a jet-boat trip through the towering cliffs of the Shotover River, has been described as one of the world's most exciting rides. Cost, including transportation from Queenstown, is $44.

Farm Visits

Dominating the opposite side of the lake are two lofty peaks—Walter Peak to the right and Mount Nicholas to the left. Both are sheep and cattle ranches. A half-day trip to Walter Peak Station by launch, the only means of access, is worthwhile. Hosts explain how the steep hills are farmed and how trained sheep dogs are able to muster the animals from "the tops." Sheep dog demonstrations are given. Launches leave from the jetties. Departures 9:30 A.M. and 2 P.M.; NZ$24.20.

Beyond Queenstown

Obtain a free copy of *Queenstown Sightseeing and Activities Guide* from the NZTP Travel Office, 49 Shotover St.; phone 28–238. The *Guide* describes full- and half-day trips, lake excursions, river trips, scenic flights and other activities and gives prices and optional times. The NZTP office can also make sightseeing reservations and arrange onward travel and accommodations.

Another useful and convenient center for obtaining information, as well as a departure point for many sightseeing coaches, is the Mount Cook Travel Office at the bottom of the mall on the corner of Rees St.

(It is more convenient to reserve at any of the above offices than to try to contact individual operators.)

Coronet Peak

One of New Zealand's most popular ski fields, Coronet Peak, is 11 miles from Queenstown. There are no regular tours, but you can drive in your own automobile. From the road terminus at 3,800 ft. a chair lift rises 1,600 ft. to the summit, from which there are spectacular views. Coronet Peak is snow-covered only from June through September, and summer visits are worthwhile. The Coronet Cresta Run is a thrilling toboggan ride on brake-controlled sleighs down 1,800 feet of a stainless steel track.

Skippers Canyon

While highly interesting, this trip should be taken only by those with strong nerves. A warning road sign "Extreme Care Necessary" does not exaggerate. But if you go by one of the regular tour coaches it is safe, though scary. The narrow road twists around a steep gorge past abandoned gold-prospecting sites and relics to a turning point. It was from this part of the Shotover River that a great amount of gold was taken. Tours available.

Cattledrome

Just past the Edith Cavell Bridge is the Cattledrome, where cattle have been trained to walk into the large exhibition hall and mount steps to their allotted pens. Seven breeds of beef cattle and three cows of leading dairy breeds are displayed. A focal point is the milking of the cows by machine at eye level. The show includes a film, *The Grass Growers,* showing how New Zealand has led the world in developing pastures. Shows are held at 9:30 A.M. and 4:15 P.M., and tours are available.

An extension of the Cattledrome tour takes in Arrowtown, with time to explore the gold-mining/pioneer museum and preserved village. Departs 2 P.M.; NZ$31.

Trail Rides

For those who like horseback riding, the half-day trail rides operated by Moonlight Stables from Arthurs Point into the old gold-mining district of Moonlight are something unusual. Transport is by courtesy coach to and from the stables. Departures 9:30 A.M. and 2 P.M.; NZ$30 (half-day).

Trout Fishing Safaris

The lakes and rivers around Queenstown abound in rainbow and brown trout and quinnat salmon. If you're an expert you can arrange to be taken on a guided fly-fishing tour. If you're just an amateur, but would like to try your luck, you can go trolling or spinning from a jet boat. Fishing gear is supplied on all charters.

Hang-Gliding Simulator

The hang-gliding simulator enables you to fly a hang glider without the fear of falling to earth. The glider allows full freedom of flight but is safety-harnessed to a 750-ft.-long cable which descends from a 90-ft.-high hill, and the pilot is also safely strapped in. After a brief period of instruction on how to control the flight you can speed down the cable at about 20 mph until gently brought to rest at the base. The simulator is about 12 miles from Queenstown on Malagan's Rd. (the main road to Arrowtown). And transport departs at 9 A.M., 10:30 A.M., noon, 1:30 P.M., 3 P.M., and 4:30 P.M. The cost is NZ$44 an hour with a guaranteed minimum of four flights. Phone Arrowtown 343.

The Ultimate Game

The thrill of stalking an enemy (and being stalked) is realistically created in the Ultimate Game, which is played (usually by teams) in a dense pine forest interspersed with small clearings. Dressed in overalls of different colors and protective goggles, each team tries to ambush, force to surrender, or shoot its opponents with plastic-coated colored water pellets fired from a gas-powered pistol. "Casualties" report to the game controller to register points. Teams can be organized. The site is almost opposite the Arrowtown intersection on the main road to Queenstown. Courtesy transport can be provided. The cost is $18 for an average playing time of 1½ hours.

Whitewater Rafting

The swift Shotover and Kawarau rivers with their turbulent boulder-strewn stretches are ideal for whitewater rafting. The upper canyon of the Shotover River is between rock walls; the lower canyon has twists, turns, and rapids; and the Kawarau is punctuated with rapids. Trips range from 3 to 4½ hours and prices from $64 to $80. All equipment is provided. Rafting operators are Challenge Rafting, Danes Safaris, Kawarau Raft Expeditions, Queenstown Adventure Trips, and Value Tours Rafting.

Arrowtown

Just 12 miles from Queenstown, Arrowtown, now little more than a village, was once a booming gold-rush town. Its main street is lined with sycamores, which lay a golden carpet of leaves in the fall. Many of the old stone cottages and wooden buildings have been preserved and are still lived in, giving this sleepy village an air of realism while it still retains its history.

Guided Hiking

Two outstanding guided scenic hikes (known here as walks) operate from Queenstown. The Routeburn Walk covers 25 miles of track or trail over four days through Fiordland and Mount Aspiring National Parks, with accommodations and meals provided in mountain lodges. The four-day Hollyford Valley Walk is also through alpine scenery, although in a different direction. The walks are from November through April.

Queenstown to Te Anau By Road

The road follows the Frankton Arm of Lake Wakatipu to the airport and then drops gently down to the Kawarau Dam Bridge over the outlet of the lake. The dam was constructed in 1926 to lower the waters of the Kawarau River so that the alluvial gold-bearing deposits could be worked. The scheme was not successful and has long been abandoned.

For a time you follow the flanks of the Remarkables and the eastern shore of the lake before arriving at Kingston, about 30 miles from Queens-town at the southern tip of the lake.

The way then lies through the barley-growing and seed-producing region of Garston and, after passing several little settlements, descends to Five Rivers, which is little more than a gas station. Watch for the sign-posted right-hand turnoff to Te Anau, as the main highway continues to Lumsden and farther south. If you are not alert you could fly past it and add miles to your journey by having to turn inland at Lumsden. If you set your odometer at zero at Queenstown it should be reading about 60 miles (97km) at Five Rivers.

The main road from Lumsden is joined at Mossburn, 20 miles on, and a right-hand turn is made for Te Anau. Much of the journey is through rolling farm country and some tussock. On the left are the Takitimu Ranges, said in Maori legend to be the petrified hull of the canoe "Takiti-mu."

Te Anau is 118 miles (190km) from Queenstown, and it is a pleasant 2½- to 3-hour drive.

Fiordland

Some of New Zealand's most spectacular mountain and lake scenery is found in Fiordland National Park on the southwest corner of the South Island. Over three million acres in area, it is one of the largest national parks in the world, and the terrain is so precipitous and heavily forested that parts have never been explored. The land still holds secrets. In 1948 a bird long believed to be extinct, the Takahe *(notornis),* was discovered in a remote valley. It is now being nurtured to preserve the species. In 1947 a glowworm cave was discovered.

A flight over Fiordland will show why much of it is virginal. Towering peaks and sheer rock walls are jumbled together as if to keep humans at bay. The steep rock walls slide into narrow valleys, and the luxuriant rain forest is almost impenetrable.

In Dusky Sound Captain Cook rested his crew after a two-month voyage, made tea from the manuka shrub, brewed a sort of beer, and boiled a native celery plant as antidotes to scurvy. It was here, too, that the first house was built by a European, bagpipes were first played (by one of the sailors), and the first musket was fired by a Maori.

Queenstown and Te Anau are the starting points for a journey into Fiordland. The highlight is Milford Sound, which can be seen in a 1½-hour scenic flight but, to really appreciate the dramatic and outstanding scenery, you should travel by road down the eastern shore of Lake Wakatipu to Lake Te Anau and thence through the mountains to the sound.

From October through April there are full-day return trips by coach, although a one- or two-day stopover at Te Anau is well worthwhile. Alternatively, you can travel by road to Milford Sound, stay overnight, and return to Queenstown by air.

The road journey to Milford Sound is more exciting than the return, as the scenery opens before you more impressively. A two- or three-hour launch cruise down the sound should certainly be undertaken.

Milford Sound

Milford is magnificent—there is no other way of describing the primeval grandeur of this region sculptured by Nature. The majesty of the scenery makes the visitor feel insignificant.

Thousands of years ago great glaciers gouged out the land from granite rock, forming a deep basin. As the glaciers receded, the sea flowed in, filling a great depression. From the water's edge almost vertical cliffs rise several thousands of feet. They are mostly bare rock, yet here and there vegetation somehow clings to the sheer slopes. In many places valleys high above the sound end abruptly in a U shape. These are known as hanging valleys and were formed when the glaciers feeding the main glacier receded and disappeared.

Milford Sound is 10 miles long and about 1½ miles wide at its broadest point. At its deepest the floor is 1,280 ft. below sea level. So deep are the waters that the largest cruise ships can enter the sound, but there is only one place, Harrison Cove, where they can anchor.

Like a forbidding guardian, Mitre Peak rises 5,560 ft. to dominate the sound. Opposite, the Bowen Falls explodes in a great spout of water which soars high into the air before tumbling 520 feet into the sound in a flurry of spray. Farther down are the Stirling Falls (480 ft.), which flow from hanging valleys in a series of leaps before they too plunge into the sea.

A regular launch cruise helps one appreciate the majesty of Milford Sound. Only in this way can a sense of the vastness of the encircling cliff faces and the towering heights of the mountains be gained. Scenic flights are also a wonderful way to view the sound and can be arranged from Queenstown.

Milford Sound has one irritating defect—it is heavily populated with voracious sandflies, so go armed with insect repellent.

The Road to Milford Sound

The road to Milford Sound from Te Anau is probably the most scenically exciting in New Zealand and should be traveled if possible. The distance is only 75 miles, but it will take you three hours or so—not that the road is difficult or dangerous, but there are many points where you will want to stop to admire the view or take photographs.

Shortly after leaving Te Anau, the road crosses the Upukerora River, a noted trout stream, and for the 17 miles to the Te Anau Downs sheep ranch there are views of the South Fiord, Center Island and the Middle Fiord. The road then enters the Eglinton Valley and follows the Eglinton

River for some miles. A magnificent forest of beech trees, some from 70 to 90 ft. high, flanks the road between the serrated peaks of the Earl Range on the left and the Livingstone Range on the right.

Suddenly, you enter the Avenue of the Disappearing Mountain. At the end of a long avenue of beech trees a mountain slowly disappears from view instead of growing larger as one would expect. This effect is caused by an almost imperceptible rise in the road and is startling, to say the least.

From Cascade Creek Camp, 47 miles (69.5km) from Te Anau, the outstanding beauty of Fiordland begins. Two small forest-ringed lakes, Gunn and Fergus, are passed, and then the divide is reached. As you round a big bend the Crosscut Range comes into view. A little farther on Mt. Christina, over 7,000 ft., suddenly appears, its sparkling peak rising above the skyline framed by forest.

High, stark granite cliffs, snow-capped and laced with waterfalls, close in as the road follows the floor of the Hollyford Valley and gradually climbs to a large basin.

Like a pinpoint in the massive barrier, the portal of the Homer Tunnel appears. The construction of the tunnel was a daunting undertaking. In winter the area is subject to mountain avalanches. Twisted hunks of reinforced concrete testify to their destructive force where a protective canopy was caught in an avalanche and crumped out of recognition. There is little danger, however, as the road is closed when there is a possibility of avalanches.

Although it is perfectly safe, the tunnel appears a little fearsome at first sight. There is no graceful facade—it is simply a hole in the rock. Its walls are of rough-hewn rock and there is no lighting. Headlights have to be used, and the traffic is one-way for 25 minutes of each hour. When almost at the center you can hear the roar of a hidden waterfall.

The Homer Tunnel is 3,000 ft. above sea level at its eastern portal and descends for three-quarters of a mile at a grade of 1 in 10. It is only 12 ft. high and 22 ft. wide. As you emerge from the tunnel it is as if the backdrop of a stage were being raised to reveal the beautiful Cleddau Valley.

The road snakes down the moraine in a series of zig-zags and, still dropping, follows the floor of the valley, flanked by lovely forest and occasional waterfalls. The towering mountains of the Sheerdown Range, Mt. Underwood, the Barrier Range and Barren Peak almost enclose the valley. From Tutoko Bridge there are fine views of Mt. Tutoko (9,042 ft.). Then, as you round a corner, Milford Sound springs suddenly into view, like a slide being projected onto a screen.

The Milford Track

"The finest walk in the world" is the description often given to this five-day, 33-mile hike from Te Anau to Milford Sound. It was not until 1888 that a Scottish immigrant, Quintin Mackinnon, discovered a mountain pass that made land access possible to Milford Sound. This route is now one of the most popular hikes in New Zealand, if only because of the spectacular scenery through which it passes.

The walk is a 5-day hike, with an average of 6.5 miles per day, with comfortable overnight accommodation in well-equipped huts. With a guide, it is taken in easy increments and is within the capabilities of anyone who is reasonably fit and used to walking. The season is from November to April. As parties are restricted to 40 persons, reservations are necessary.

The lake launch leaves Te Anau in the early afternoon and takes you to the head of the lake, from which a half-mile bush track leads to Glade House, where the first night is spent.

The first section of the Milford Track has been likened to a Sunday-afternoon stroll, for the path is broad and rises only 500 ft. in 10 miles. After crossing the swing-bridge over the Clinton River you follow the river through the Clinton Canyon. On the left are the Pariroa Heights, which reach 5,000 ft. For the last mile of the journey the saddle of the Mackinnon Pass can be seen framed in the converging walls of the canyon ahead. The night is spent at Pompolona Huts.

The track becomes steeper after leaving Pompolona and the beech forests give way to ribbonwood. The bushline is left behind as you approach Mackinnon Pass, and at 3,400 ft., the saddle, the highest point in the journey is reached.

The view from the Mackinnon Pass is ample reward for the climb. Three thousand feet down on one side is the bush-clad canyon of the Arthur River, and on the other, just as sheer, is the great cleft of the Clinton Canyon, the bed of an ancient glacier, pointing the way back to Lake Te Anau. Lake Mintaro glitters far below, and the Clinton River threads its way along the valley floor, with the rock walls of the canyon towering thousands of feet on either side. More intimate beauty is provided by the subalpine flowers which grow in the pass—mountain lily and daisy and the thin wiry snowgrass make a wonderful show among the rugged hills. Descending from the pass, the track leads under several mountains and ends at Quintin Huts, where the night is spent after the 9¼ mile hike.

A sidetrip to the Sutherland Falls is normally included. The track enters the bush from beside the huts and rises gradually through beautiful ferns and beech trees. The roar of the falls steadily increases and, after a walk of a little over a mile, they come into view.

The final leg concludes with a launch journey of two miles to the jetty in Milford Sound. Most hikers travel back to Te Anau by motor coach.

Lake Te Anau

Built on the edge of the lake, the township of Te Anau is the land gateway to Fiordland and Milford Sound. At the foot of high, rugged, forest-clad mountains, the lake has three long narrow arms. It is the South Island's largest lake, being 33 miles long and six miles wide at the widest point. Its greatest depth is 906 ft., making the floor 212 ft. below sea level.

Lake Te Anau shares with Waitomo the distinction of having a glow-worm cave, but the two differ in many respects. While the Waitomo glow-worms extinguish their lights when disturbed by noise, the Te Anau glow-worms continue shining above a noisy torrent of water.

Te Anau is a contraction of the Maori name *Te Ana-au,* which means "cave of swirling water." No one knew of this cave until 1947, when Lawson Burrows, a curious resident, went exploring and entered a cavity where water was flowing out of a hill.

A visit to the cave is now an essential part of Te Anau stopovers. The trip takes about 2½ hours and can be undertaken after dinner.

The caves are reached after a half-hour launch cruise. The entrance is low, and one has to crouch for about 20 yards to reach a higher chamber where the river plunges over a human-made dam, necessary to float a steel punt. A series of concrete ramps are climbed and a second boat boarded to enter the glowworm grotto itself. As at Waitomo, the ceiling and walls are covered with thousands and thousands of brightly shining glowworms.

Lake Te Anau is a popular weekend resort for residents of the city of Invercargill, about 100 miles away, many of whom have cottages on the lake shores and boats on the waters. It is popular, too, with anglers, as its waters are full of rainbow and brown trout and Atlantic salmon.

From Te Anau, day trips can be taken by coach or hired automobile to Milford Sound, and scenic flights are also operated.

Te Anau is not far away from New Zealand's "Kentucky country," the Hokonui Hills. There were no feuds, but illicit whisky was distilled there some years ago. Objecting to paying tax on liquor, a Scottish family decided to make their own. The terrain of the hills is such that a successful surprise raid was difficult, but occasionally the "revenooers" paid a visit. They sometimes found the still, but seldom the distillers, who had quietly melted away. The story is told that on several occasions the stills were dismantled and sold to recover costs. And who bought them? The distillers, of course, who took the parts back to the hills for reassembly and went happily back to distilling. Older residents still talk about the potent Hokonui whisky.

The crude but distinctive label featured a skull and crossbones with the words:

> Ergo Bibamus
> Free from all Poisons
> OLD HOKONUI
> Passed All Tests except the Police
> Bottled by ME for YOU
> Produce of SOUTHLAND
> Supplied to all Snake Charmers

You might be able to pick up a label—but not the whisky. Full-day coach trips to Milford Sound are operated by H&H Group (phone 27–146) and NZR Road Services (phone 725–599). Fiordland Travel Services (phone 7416) runs 2 ¼-hour afternoon and evening trips to the Te Anau glowworm caves.

Lake Manapouri

"The lake of the sorrowing heart" is the meaning of the Maori name. The legend tells of two sisters who, near death in the high forests, held each other and wept. Their tears divided the hills and formed the lake.

Flanked by the Cathedral Mountains, it is studded with small islands clad in native bush. It has many moods. On a clear morning or in the late afternoon it can be peaceful and serene, with the tranquil beauty of its surroundings mirrored in the waters and the stillness broken only by the call of the tui or bellbird. Or it can have an air of mystery when lying beneath a curtain of mist.

Lake Manapouri is long and narrow. With a coastline of over 100 miles, it is 20 miles long and six miles wide at its widest point, and the deepest part is 872 ft. below sea level. Rainbow and brown trout and Atlantic salmon are plentiful in the lake.

Lake Manapouri became the focal point in one of New Zealand's most heated controversies over the environment. Some 10 years ago the government decided to divert some of the lake waters to a power house, mainly to produce the large amount of electricity required by a new aluminum smelter 100 miles away. This meant raising the level of the lake by several feet to provide water storage, thus burying vegetation at the water's edge and submerging some of the small beaches. A vociferous and effective body, the Guardians of the Lake, was formed, and a petition with some 265,000 signatures was presented to Parliament. The battle was not completely won, but significant modifications were made to the plan.

The hydroelectric plant is unusual in that the powerhouse is 700 ft. underground. The lake waters are channeled down into the powerhouse and discharged into Doubtful Sound on the west coast of the island. Fiordland Travel Services runs a four-hour trip which is full of beauty and interest. Leaving the natural boat anchorage at Pearl Harbor, near the Manapouri township, the launch *Fiordland* threads its way through the islands to West Arm. From here passengers are taken by coach down a 1¼-mile road, which spirals down to the powerhouse 700 ft. below. The powerhouse is a cavern hewn out of solid rock, 364 ft. long by 59 ft. wide. The water drawn from the lake falls nearly 600 ft. to turn the turbines and then passes through a 6¼-mile tailrace to discharge in Deep Cove in Doubtful Sound.

The Helicopter Line operates regular sightseeing flights from Manapouri over the 2,200-foot Wilmot Pass into Doubtful Sound and Deep Cove. Cost is NZ$198.

Invercargill

Invercargill (population 50,000) is New Zealand's southernmost city. The Maoris called it Murihiku ("the end of the tail"). The name is formed from the combination of "Inver," from the Gaelic "mouth of the river," and "Cargill," after Captain William Cargill, the first superintendent of the province of Otago. Most of the settlers were of Scottish descent and have left their mark on those streets named after Scottish rivers or places.

For 30 years Invercargill was a "dry" area, a prohibition city where no liquor could be sold. Some 25 years ago it went "wet" in an experiment that has now been followed in several parts of New Zealand. Instead of allowing private enterprise to establish liquor stores, a licensing trust was formed, and all profits are devoted to improving the city's amenities.

For many years the southland area was the largest oat-producing region in New Zealand but, now that the horse has been replaced by machinery, it concentrates on sheep raising and dairying. Four large meat-packing plants process nearly six million lambs annually, most of which are exported from the port of Bluff, 17 miles to the south, where an 84-acre island was built in the harbor to provide docks and loading facilities. Across the harbor a large smelter produces 110,000 tons of aluminum annually, powered by electricity from Lake Manapouri.

Fifteen miles across the restless waters of Foveaux Strait lies Stewart Island, New Zealand's third and most southerly island. Stewart Island is so small and sparsely populated that even New Zealanders are inclined to overlook it and forget that New Zealand comprises three and not two islands. It has a population of less than 400, concentrated in one area, and only about 16 miles of road. Rugged and heavily forested, it is indented with many lovely bays and beaches and is a bird sanctuary. The Maoris called the island *Rakiura* ("sky glow") from the superb sunsets for which it is famed.

Off the coast, mutton birds (sooty shearwaters) are harvested in April and May. The birds are very fatty and have a very strong fishy taste.

Not so, however, the large, plump Stewart Island oysters dredged from the waters of Foveaux Strait. They are much larger than rock oysters and perhaps not as sweet but, if oysters are your dish, you'll find a dozen almost a full meal. They are marketed throughout New Zealand, but there is a special gastronomical joy in eating oysters freshly dredged from the strait.

DUNEDIN

Dunedin shows a Scottish influence. The original plan of the new Edinburgh to be founded in Otago was made by the lay association of the Free Church of Scotland. It was to be a truly Scots settlement where the Kirk would be the basis of community life.

Like Christchurch, the city was surveyed and laid out before the colonists arrived. The surveyor was instructed to reproduce features of the Scottish capital, and Dunedin has as many associations for the Scots as Christchurch has for the English. Many of the streets bear familiar names—Princes, George, King, Hanover, Frederick, Castle, and Queen streets—and the little boulder-strewn stream flowing through the northeast corner of the city is called the Water of Leith.

In the early 1880s gold was discovered in the province. Thousands of prospectors poured in from all over New Zealand and from Britain, Australia, and even California. Dunedin's population jumped from 2,000 to 5,000 and the population of the Otago Province from 12,000 to 75,000.

Dunedin was the center where prospectors met and prepared to leave for the gold fields. The township became blocked with shanties and tents pitched on any vacant spot. Miners swarmed down every track leading to the gold fields, traveling by bullock wagon, on horseback, and on foot. As much as $200 a week (a substantial sum in those days) could be made and, in the first four wild years, Otago exported $14,000,000 worth of gold.

Dunedin boomed. But even in the middle of this dizzy prosperity the canny Scots citizens gave thought to the future and, when inevitably the boom ended, the settlement had something permanent to show for the years of precarious good fortune.

The citizens needed all their determination and resourcefulness in the years that followed, for they had to find new and more permanent means of making their living. They established flourishing industries and developed fruit growing and farming in the province. New prosperity was found after the first shipment of frozen meat left Port Chalmers in 1882.

Today Dunedin has a population of about 120,000 and is New Zealand's fifth largest city. Its progress has been steady, if less spectacular, over the last three-quarters of a century. Stone buildings replaced the wooden shanties of gold-boom times, and Dunedin's beautiful churches and schools are among the finest in the country.

First Church, Gothic in design, stands in Moray Place right in the center of the city, and when the spire is floodlit the building is an impressive sight. St. Paul's Cathedral dominates the Octagon. The main block of the Otago University, the oldest university in New Zealand, is also Gothic; a stately gray stone building with a tall clock tower.

Railroad Station

Railroad enthusiasts will find the railroad station fun ("railway" is the New Zealand term). Its architect was dubbed Gingerbread George, and the station is a fitting monument to him. He seems to have wanted to leave nothing undecorated. Heraldic lions corner the massive copper-capped tower, the NZR (New Zealand Railways) cypher is engraved on window panes everywhere, ornate scrolls surround the ticket-office windows, and stained-glass windows depict locomotives approaching at full steam.

Lanarch Castle

Built in 1871 and copied from an old Scottish castle, Lanarch Castle is a living memento of the Victorian way of life. William Lanarch had married the daughter of a French duke and, being wealthy, he set out to provide her with the sort of lavish home he thought she should have. It is said to have cost about $300,000, which was a very considerable sum in those days. The interior is a mass of ornate carving and mosaics, elaborately decorated ceilings, and marble fireplaces. The most notable feature is a Georgian hanging staircase. There is even a dungeon, where Lanarch is said to have locked up poachers caught on the property. It is situated on the Otago Peninsula, nine miles from the city, and is included in sightseeing tours or can be visited by taxi or private automobile.

Olveston

This stately mansion, built between 1904 and 1906, stands in a beautiful setting of trees and formal gardens. In the Dutch-influenced Jacobean style, Olveston has some 35 rooms, and contains an unusual collection of domestic art: paintings, ceramics, ivory, bronze, silverware, and furniture. It is only one mile from the city.

Royal Albatross Colony

Taiaroa Head, at the tip of the Otago Peninsula about an hour's journey from the city, is the only place in the world where this magnificent bird breeds close to human habitation and can be seen at close quarters. One of the largest of birds, it has a wing span of about 11 ft., weighs up to 15 pounds, stands about 30 inches high, has a bill about 7 inches long, and may live 70 years. It does not breed until it is about seven years old and then only on alternate years.

The birds arrive from their migration in September and settle down to lay a single egg, which is white, is about 5 inches long, and weighs about a pound. The parents share sitting duty for about 11 weeks, and the chick may take three days to struggle free from the shell. It is not fully fledged for about a year, when it flies as far as Tahiti in search of squid. Eight years pass before it returns to start a new breeding cycle.

The colony is rigidly protected and bookings must be made in advance through the NZTP Travel Office, 131 Princes St., phone (024) 740–344; parties are restricted to 10 persons. The season is usually late November through mid-March but may be canceled without notice to protect the birds. There is no public transport, so you may need a taxi or rental car. From January, when the chicks have hatched, there is an afternoon coach tour, usually on Mondays, Wednesdays, and Saturdays only.

Weather conditions at the colony are often boisterous, and 40 to 50 knot winds are not unusual. Warm clothing and walking shoes are recommended. Binoculars are available for observing the birds.

The Roads to the West Coast

Like a long spine, the Southern Alps divide the west from the east coast. There are only three ways across them—the Lewis Pass and Arthur's Pass from Christchurch or the Haast Pass from Queenstown and Wanaka.

By the Lewis Pass, the northern route, it is 208 miles (335km) to Greymouth. The ascent to and descent from the 2,840-ft. summit lie through glorious beech forests.

By Arthur's Pass it is 159 miles (258km) to Greymouth. The first pass to be negotiated is Porter's Pass which, at 3,102 ft., is 77 ft. higher than Arthur's Pass on the main divide. It is the boundary between Canterbury and Westland and the center of Arthur's Pass National Park. The mountains are pierced by a 5¼-mile railroad tunnel, an outstanding engineering feat. One portal appears at Otira as you leave the pass.

Neither pass poses difficulties to the driver, although the descent from the summit of Arthur's Pass to the west coast is winding and steep.

The Haast Pass, at 1,849 ft., is the lowest of the alpine passes and many find it more restful to the eye. The road passes through beautiful forest and mountain scenery, with good views of Mount Brewster (8,264 ft.) and the Brewster Glacier. As there is no settlement of any size between Wanaka and the Fox Glacier 180 miles away, take a picnic lunch.

The opening of the Haast Pass road in 1965 has opened a circular route from Christchurch through to the West Coast, to the glaciers and through the Haast Pass to Queenstown. Before then it was necessary to return from the glaciers to Greymouth in order to reach Queenstown.

Franz Josef and Fox Glaciers

The main attractions of the west coast are the Franz Josef Glacier and the Fox Glacier, which flow down from the Southern Alps. Only 24 miles apart, they are the lowest in the southern hemisphere and are unusual in that they descend to the edge of native forest. Both have receded in recent years, but the recession does not make them less beautiful. Scenic roads lead almost to the terminal faces, from which you can take a guided walk on the ice if conditions are suitable. Boots are provided by the hotel. The walk at the Franz Josef is now quite a rugged one.

The Franz Josef Glacier was named after the Emperor Franz Josef of Austria by the geologist Sir Julius von Haast in 1862.

The glacier's broken surface ends abruptly in a terminal ridge. Here the ice beneath the covering shingle is gray, but only a short distance above it is clear white. From an ice cave at the foot of the glacier the turbulent Waiho River ("smoky water") gushes out and flows for 12 miles to the coast. The water appears milky from the particles of rock ground to dust by the glacier, and a layer of mist sits above the surface, formed by the sudden chilling of the warm air as it meets the ice-cold river. A short distance from the source of the river is a small hot mineral spring, which emerges beside cold water.

The glaciers start at the crests of the Southern Alps and are fed by heavy snowfalls brought by westerly winds. The steep mountain slopes account for the glacier's precipitous fall—about 1,000 ft. a mile.

Unlike other New Zealand glaciers, the Franz Josef's surface is almost clear of debris. The surface is marked by deep crevasses and jagged pinnacles, owing to tension caused by the more rapid motion of the middle of the glacier or by its movement over steep slopes in the rock floor of the valley. The crevasses are usually confined to the upper layers of the ice where the pressure is not great enough to force the ice to flow.

Ice is solid, but the movement of a glacier resembles that of a viscous fluid. The movement of the Franz Josef Glacier varies from 1½ to 15 ft. a day.

Be sure to visit the small church in the bush, St. James Chapel. A large window behind the altar gives a magnificent view of the bush and mountains.

Aerial sightseeing trips are run from the air strip, and ski planes are used for landings on the glacier snowfields.

The Fox Glacier was named as a compliment to Sir William Fox, who visited it during his term as premier of the colony. The Fox River emerges from the terminal face and flows westward to join the Cook River on its journey to the sea. The Cook River Flat is good sheep and cattle country.

Nearby Lake Matheson is famous for its reflections of Mt. Cook and Mt. Tasman. The best time to see these is in the early morning. The return walk through the native bush surrounding the lake takes about 40 minutes.

Hokitika

Hokitika now has a population of only a little more than 3,000, but in 1864 and 1865 it was a booming gold-rush town of thousands. In those years over 1.3 million ounces of gold were exported. But the rush declined as quickly as it had begun when rich deposits were exhausted. Although small quantities of gold may still be found, Hokitika now mainly relies on farming and lumber.

But it was left with one natural asset—greenstone, a type of jade. New Zealand Greenstone, as it is called, is found in rivers near Hokitika, and helicopters are used to bring out boulders from inaccessible sites in the mountains. A 12-ton boulder was recently dragged from the sea.

Greenstone is extremely hard and can be cut only by diamond saws. The Maoris called it *pounamu* and used to raid the area to obtain it for their war clubs and ornaments. A visit to the Westland Greenstone Factory to watch the stone being cut, fashioned, and polished is well worthwhile. Greenstone jewelry and ornaments may be purchased at the factory (as in most souvenir shops throughout New Zealand) but, like other kinds of jade, it is not inexpensive.

Hokitika is also a prime source for a popular New Zealand delicacy—whitebait. A type of smelt, it is netted in spring at the mouths of and on the banks of rivers as it swims upstream. The fish is usually cooked in batter as fritters or patties.

Greymouth

Greymouth, with a population of just under 8,000, is primarily a coal-mining town and the main business center of the west coast. Seven miles south is Shantytown, a convincing replica of a gold-field town at the height of the boom. Authenticity has been observed as far as possible, in both the buildings and the replicas on display. Some of the buildings were restored from those actually used, and an 1897 locomotive hauls a couple of passenger cars a short distance through the bush.

Traces of gold are still found in the area, and you can try your luck in panning for gold at Shantytown. Even if you don't find a nugget, which occasionally happens, you can be reasonably sure of leaving with a few glittering specks in a tiny vial of water. Transport can be arranged through the West Coast Public Relations Office, Mawhera Quay; phone 5101.

Marlborough Sounds

North of Christchurch and at the northern tip of the South Island are the Marlborough Sounds, an enormous jigsaw puzzle of sunken valleys forming over 600 miles of waterways. Three of the largest are Queen Charlotte, Pelorus, and Kenepuru sounds, Pelorus being the most extensive (34 miles long). The hills, headlands, and peninsulas rising from the sheltered waters are in many cases densely wooded, and everywhere there are secluded bays and beaches. Some of the hills have been turned into sheep farms which can only be reached by water.

Understandably, the sounds are a popular holiday center for both Wellington and Christchurch residents for, although they are 217 miles (339.5km) by road from Christchurch, they are only 52 miles from Wellington by sea. The opportunities for swimming, sailing, boating, and exciting sea fishing are limitless. Those who like the amenities of a township will base themselves at Picton (population normally about 3,000, but rising to 10,000 at the height of the holiday season between Christmas and the end of January); those who prefer relaxing in quiet scenic beauty by the sea "away from it all," or enjoy boat fishing or surf-casting, will choose a place like the Portage in Kenepuru Sound.

The ubiquitous Captain Cook entered Queen Charlotte Sound in 1770 and anchored his ship *Endeavour* near the northern entrance in "a very safe and convenient cove" (Ship Cove). On an island he hoisted the flag and announced he was taking possession of New Zealand in the name of King George III, after whose queen the sound is named. Cook returned to the sound four times.

Passenger-vehicle ships of over 4,000 tons sail regularly each day from Wellington to Picton. The voyage takes 3½ hours, but only two hours are spent in Cook Strait itself. The last hour is entrancing. After the steamer has swung through a narrow entrance it cruises down the sound, the banks of which are dotted with sheep farms.

From Picton there are launch cruises to various parts of the sound and organized fishing trips.

Nelson

Only 40 minutes by air from Wellington and 73 miles by road from Picton, Nelson is one of the sunniest places in New Zealand, with 2,407 sunshine hours a year. Its climate and lovely beaches make it highly popular for holidays and retirement.

In 1858, although it had a population of less than 3,000, Nelson was declared a city by Queen Victoria when she ordained that it should be a bishop's see. A cathedral was duly built. Today Nelson has a population of over 44,000.

Nelson is the hub of one of New Zealand's largest fruit-growing areas. Orchards are to be seen everywhere, and it exports over a million cases of apples each year, mainly to Britain. It is here, too, that New Zealand's tobacco is grown, as well as hops for brewing.

Nelson is proud of being the birthplace of Lord Rutherford, the first man to split the atom. He received his early education at Nelson College and went on to do research into radioactivity at McGill University, Montreal, and later at Cambridge University, England. He was born at Brightwater, 12 miles south of Nelson.

Near outlying Takaka is one of the largest fresh water springs in the world, Pupu Springs. Water bubbles out of the sand at a reputed 200 million gallons a day and a constant temperature of 52°F.

PRACTICAL INFORMATION FOR THE SOUTH ISLAND

ACCOMMODATIONS. Average room rates for hotels on the South Island run NZ$85–NZ$145; motels are slightly less expensive, averaging about NZ$60. Our price categories for a double-occupancy room, inclusive of the new 10% goods and services tax, are as follows: *deluxe,* NZ$165 and up; *expensive,* NZ$100–NZ$165; *moderate,* NZ$70–NZ$100; *inexpensive,* under NZ$65. THC, where marked below, indicates an establishment of the Tourist Hotel Corporation, which has high-Quality Rooms in the remoter areas.

Christchurch

Latimer Motor Lodge. *Deluxe.* 30 Latimer Sq.; (03) 796–760. 53 rooms. Restaurant, bars, parking.

Noah's Hotel. *Deluxe.* Corner Worcester St. and Oxford Terr.; (03) 794–700. 214 rooms; some suites. Restaurants, bars.

Avon Hotel. *Expensive.* 356 Oxford Terr.; (03) 791–180. 108 rooms. Restaurant, bars, parking.

Chateau Regency. *Expensive.* 187–189 Deans Ave.; (03) 488–999. 93 rooms; suites available. Restaurant, bars, parking.

Christchurch Airport TraveLodge. *Expensive.* Corner Memorial Ave. and Orchard Rd.; (03) 583–139. 150 rooms. Restaurants, bar, parking, pool.

Commodore Airport Hotel. *Expensive.* 447 Memorial Ave.; (03) 588–129. 105 rooms. Restaurant, bars, close to airport and putting greens.

Cotswold Inn. *Expensive.* 88–90 Papanui Rd.; (03) 553–535. Unusual hotel, with six wings built to resemble a 16th-century inn. 50 luxury suites. Restaurants, bars, parking.

The Elms. *Expensive.* 458 Papanui Rd.; (03) 553–577. 76 units. Pool, restaurant, video in rooms.

The George Hotel. *Expensive.* 50 Park Terr.; (03) 794–560. 69 rooms, all with TV, video, and private facilities.

Vacation Inn. *Expensive.* 776 Colombo St.; (03) 795–880. 90 rooms. Restaurants, bars.

Australasia Motor Inn. *Moderate.* Corner Hereford and Barbadoes sts.; (03) 790–540. 25 rooms. Restaurant, parking, video in rooms.

Canterbury Inn. *Moderate.* 110 Mandeville St.; (03) 485–049. 45 rooms. Restaurant, bar, parking.

Coker's Hotel. *Moderate.* 52 Manchester St.; (03) 798–580. 37 rooms. Restaurant, bars.

Redwood Inn. *Moderate.* 340 Main North Rd.; (03) 529–165. 28 rooms. Restaurant, bars, parking.

Russley Hotel. *Moderate.* Roydale Ave.; (03) 588–289. 69 rooms. Restaurant, bar, pool, golf course adjacent.

Shirley Lodge Motor Hotel. *Moderate.* 112 Marshlands Rd.; (03) 853–034. 63 rooms. Bar, restaurant, parking.

Stonehurst Hotel. *Moderate.* 241 Gloucester St.; (03) 794–620. 50 rooms, all with private facilities. Game room, TV lounge.

Dunedin

Abbey Motor Lodge. *Expensive.* 680 Castle St.; (024) 775–380. 38 rooms, 12 motel apartments. Restaurant, bar, parking.

Pacific Park Motor Inn. *Expensive.* 21–24 Wallace St.; (024) 773–374. 59 rooms, restaurant, bar.

Leisure Lodge Motor Inn. *Moderate.* Corner Great King and Duke sts.; (024) 775–360. 50 rooms. Restaurant, bar.

Quality Inn. *Moderate.* 20 Smith St.; (024) 776–784. 55 rooms. Restaurant, bar.
Regal Court. *Moderate.* 755 George St.; (024) 777–729; 12 motel flats in different ethnic styles; parking.
Southern Cross Hotel. *Moderate.* Corner High and Princes sts.; (024) 770–752. 73 rooms. Restaurant, bars.
Adrian Motel. *Inexpensive.* 101 Queens Dr., St. Kilda (close to beach); (024) 52–009. 17 units. Kitchens, video in rooms.
Alcala Motor Lodge. *Inexpensive.* Corner George and St. David sts.; (024) 779–073. 22 motel flats; parking.
Commodore Luxury Motel. *Inexpensive.* 932 Cumberland St.; (024) 777–766. 12 motel units. Attractive decor, parking, close to restaurants.

Franz Josef Glacier

THC Franz Joseph Hotel. *Moderate.* Phone 719, Franz Joseph. 46 rooms. Restaurant, bars, parking.
Westland Motor Inn. *Moderate.* Hwy. 6, Box 33; phone 729, Franz Joseph. 97 rooms. Restaurant, bar, parking.

Fox Glacier

Golden Glacier Motor Inn. *Moderate.* Box 32; phone 847, 75 units. TV, video lounge.
Alpine View Motel. *Inexpensive.* At Fox Glacier Motor Camp; phone 821. Five units sleeping up to six.

Greymouth

Ashley Motel & Motor Inn. *Moderate.* 70–74 Tasman St.; (027) 5135. 61 units. Restaurant, bar, parking.
Recreation Hotel. *Moderate.* 68 High St.; (027) 5154. 31 rooms. Restaurant, bar, disco.
Revington's Hotel. *Moderate.* Tainui St.; (027) 7055. 32 rooms. Restaurant, bar.
West Coast Country Lodge. *Moderate.* 88 Mawhera Quay; (027) 5085. 123 rooms. Restaurant, bar, pool, parking.

Hokitika

Hotel Westland. *Moderate.* 2 Weld St. phone 411. 28 rooms. Restaurant, bar, parking; close to railway terminal.
Hokitika Motel. *Inexpensive.* 22 Fitzherbert St.; phone 292. 3 rooms; 13 units with kitchens. Breakfast available.

Invercargill

Ascot Park Hotel/Motel. *Expensive.* Corner Tay St. and Racecourse Rd.; (021) 76–195. 77 units. Spa, heated indoor pool, restaurant, bar, parking.
Grand Hotel. *Moderate.* 76 Dee St.; (021) 88–059. 62 rooms. Restaurant, bar.
Kelvin Hotel. *Moderate.* 16 Kelvin St.; (021) 82–829. 82 rooms. Restaurant, bars.
Swan Lake Motor Inn. *Moderate.* 217 North Rd.; (021) 59–135. 15 motel-type rooms, restaurant.
Don Lodge Motor Hotel. *Inexpensive.* 77 Don St.; (021) 86–125. 23 rooms. Restaurant, bar, parking.

Marlborough Sounds

The Portage Hotel. *Expensive.* Kenepuru Rd.; (057) 34–309. 26 rooms. Restaurant, bar, parking; on beachfront.
The Hotel Picton. *Moderate.* Waikawa Rd., Picton; (057) 37–202. 33 units. Boating available. Pool, restaurant, bar, parking.
Whaler's Inn. *Moderate.* Waikawa Rd.; Picton; (057) 37–002. 34 rooms. Restaurant, bar, parking.
DB Terminus Hotel. *Inexpensive.* High St., Picton; (057) 36–452. 17 rooms. Restaurant, bar, parking.

Milford Sound

THC Milford. *Expensive.* Milford Sound; phone 6, telex 4300 or cable WEL-COME. 36 rooms. At the head of the sound; well-appointed and comfortable. Restaurant, bar.

Mount Cook

THC The Hermitage. *Expensive.* Mount Cook; (0562) 809, or cable WEL-COME. 104 rooms. The best of the resort hotels, with excellent views of Mount Cook and surrounding peaks. Restaurants, bars, parking. Reservations essential.

THC Glencoe Lodge, Mount Cook Motels, and **Mount Cook Chalets.** *Moderate.* Mount Cook; (0562) 809, telex 4308, or cable WELCOME. Three less luxurious THC properties. Reservations essential.

Nelson

Quality Inn Hotel. *Moderate.* Trafalgar Square; (054) 82–299. 115 rooms. Restaurant, bar, pool, parking.

Queenstown

A-Line Motor Inn. *Expensive.* 27 Stanley St.; (0294) 27–700. 74 rooms. Restaurant, bar, lake view.

Kingsgate. *Expensive.* Frankton Rd.; (0294) 27–940. 90 rooms. Top quality.

Lakeland Regency. *Expensive.* Lake Esplanade; (0294) 27–600. 182 rooms. Restaurant, bar.

THC Remarkables Resort. *Expensive.* Yewlett Crescent; (0294) 27–150. 88 rooms. Five miles from Queenstown, near airport; restaurant, bars.

The Terraces. *Expensive.* Corner Frankton Rd. and Suburb St.; (0294) 27–950. New luxury hotel with 85 rooms. Restaurants, bar.

TraveLodge. *Expensive.* Beach St.; (0294) 27–800. 140 rooms. On lake shore; restaurant, bar, parking, sauna.

Country Lodge. *Moderate.* Fernhill Rd., ½ mile from town; (0294) 27–890. 91 rooms. Restaurant, bar, parking.

Mountain View Lodge Motel. *Inexpensive.* Frankton Rd.; (0294) 28–246. 67 units. A mile from town; restaurant, bar, parking.

Te Anau and Manapouri

Fiordland Motor Lodge. *Expensive.* Hwy. 94; (0229) 7511. 127 rooms, motel flats. Restaurant, bar, parking.

Luxmore Motor Lodge. *Expensive.* Milford Rd.; (0229) 7526. 93 rooms. Restaurant, bar, parking.

THC Te Anau Hotel. *Expensive.* Lakefront; (0229) 7411. 110 rooms. Restaurant, bars, parking.

Vacation Inn. *Expensive.* Te Anau Terr.; (0229) 7421. 95 rooms. Restaurant, bar, parking, spa; summer resort.

Campbell Autolodge. *Moderate.* 42–44 Te Anau Terr.; phone (0229) 7546. 10 units. Kitchens, parking.

Village Inn. *Moderate.* Mokoroa St.; (0229) 7911. 42 rooms, restaurant, bar, parking.

RESTAURANTS. Dinners on the South Island range from NZ$15 to NZ$30 per person for a three-course meal, not including drinks, tax, tip, though the most elegant restaurants can run higher. Many restaurants do not have liquor licenses but will allow you to bring your own wine; call ahead if this is a concern. Major credit cards are usually accepted.

Christchurch

Aggie's. 263 Bealey Ave.; 798–660. Award-winning restaurant in a century-old building.

Chambers Restaurant. 109 Cambridge Terr.; 795–634. Modern French cuisine in a former public library.

Dux de Lux. 41 Hereford St.; 66–919. A busy, trendy spot for gourmet vegetarian cuisine; alfresco tables in summer.

Forget-Me-Not. 12 Wakefield St.; 266–501. Dishes range from Mediterranean to local favorites; courtyard dining and jazz bands in summer.

Guardsman Restaurant. 103 Armagh St.; 68–701. Cozy atmosphere featuring a steak bar.

Henry Africa's. 325 Stanmore Rd.; 893–619. Nearly 30 main courses are offered in this bustling restaurant.

Kurashiki. Colombo and Gloucester sts.; 67–092. Authentic Japanese decor, food, and kimono-clad waitresses.

Leinster. 158 Leinster Rd.; 588–866. Varied game food in a warm and casual atmosphere.

Michael's. 178 High St.; 60–822. Persian decor, Mediterranean specialties.

Off the Wall. 834 Colombo St.; 797–808. Stylish atmosphere, interesting dishes.

Sign of the Takahe. Cashmere Rd.; 324–052. Wonderful city views, fireplaces, silver service, and good traditional dishes in an old stone building that resembles a small castle.

Sorbonne. Arts Centre, Rolleston Ave.; 50–566. French Provincial and New Zealand cuisine, outdoor dining in summer.

Waitangi Room. Noah's Hotel, Oxford Terr.; 794–700. Excellent food and efficient formal service in one of the country's top hotel restaurants.

Dunedin

95 Filleul. Filleul St.; 777–233. Elegant tableware, fireplaces, and dishes with a nouvelle touch.

Blades. 450 George St.; 776–548. Simple, intimate; excellent French food.

Carnarvon Station. Prince of Wales Hotel, 47A Princes St.; 770–389. Impressive, authentic railroad setting.

La Scala. Alton Ave., Musselburgh; 54–555. Attractively furnished, specializes in Italian food.

Lucerna. 218 George St.; 770–612. One of Dunedin's older restaurants, serving Mediterranean fare.

Savoy. 50 Princes St.; 778–977. Victorian-style furnishings, specializes in New Zealand foods.

Terrace Cafe. 118 Moray Pl.; 740–686. Small and quaint; specializes in vegetarian dishes.

Invercargill

Birds of a Feather. 38 Dee St.; 83–551. A small cafe, popular with locals, serving fresh seafood, produce, chicken, and homemade soups.

Crawford House. 40 Don St.; 84–776. Fresh seafood, pastas, soups.

Donovan Licensed Restaurant. 220 Bainfield St.; 58–156. Traditional dishes in an old house-turned-restaurant.

Gerrard's Restaurant. Corner Leven and Esk sts.; 83–406. Beautifully restored Queen Anne decor. Excellent seafood dishes.

Queenstown

Black Forest Inn. 100 Frankton Rd. 27–629. A small restaurant featuring hearty German specialties.

Gourmet Express. 60 Shotover St.; 29–619. American-style coffee shop, open 7 A.M. to 9 P.M. for breakfast, lunch, dinner. Good food, very moderate.

HMS Britannia. The Mall; 29–600. Seafood and game in a nautical setting.

Host Harvey Resort. Franklin Rd.; 23–540. Area specialties. All tables overlook Lake Wakatipu.

Libby's Restaurant. 27 Stanley St.; 27–700. Modern decor, candlelight, and a wide selection of a la carte meat dishes.

Packer's Arms. About four miles from Queenstown; 28–999. Genuine old stone cottage tastefully decorated; venison ragout a specialty.

Roaring Meg's Restaurant. 57 Shotover St.; 29–676. Informal atmosphere; specializes in scallops, salmon, whitebait, venison, and lamb.

Shrimps. Corner Frankton Rd. and Suburb St.; 27–950. A specialty restaurant serving fresh New Zealand seafood.

Skyline Restaurant. Top of cableway; 27–860. Panoramic views and good cuisine, including five-course buffet.

Treetops. Sunshine Bay; 27–238. Seafood specialties and an excellent lake view.

Upstairs/Downstairs. Arcade in center of town; 28–290. Modern restaurant with semi-Victorian decor.

Westy's. Center of town in the mall. Gourmet food, yet casual atmosphere.

Te Anau

Kepler's Restaurant. Corner Milford Rd. and Mokonui St.; 7909. Game and seafood.

MacKinnon Restaurant. Te Anau Terrace, in the THC Te Anau; 7411. Elegant local and French dishes.

GETTING AROUND. Christchurch. The Christchurch international and domestic airport is seven miles from the city center. Taxis are available from outside the terminal, and the average cost to a city hotel or motel is NZ$18. *Pacific Tourways* operates a shuttle service, costing NZ$2.50, to the main hotels and motels, with a pickup service on request for airline departures.

The principal taxi firms are *Blue Star Taxis* (799–799) and *Gold Band Taxis* (795–795).

Dunedin. The Momana Airport is 18.5 miles (30km) from the city. An airport bus costs NZ$6 per person each way, and buses depart and arrive opposite the Southern Cross Hotel, High St.

For taxis, phone *City Taxis* (771–771) or *Dunedin Taxis* (777–777).

Invercargill. *Blue Star Taxis* (86–079).

Queenstown. *Taxis* (27–888).

TOURS. Christchurch. *Red Bus Scenic Tours* (Christchurch Transport Board; 794–600) offers a two-hour tour of city highlights, 10 A.M. daily, Oct. to May, $11. 3-hour hills and harbor tour, including Summit Rd. and short cruise, 1:30 P.M. daily, NZ$14. 3-hour tour of Orana Park Wildlife Reserve, daily at noon, NZ$12. All tours depart from kiosk, Cathedral Square.

Canterbury Scenic Tours (69–660); half-day city-sights tour, 9 A.M. and 1:30 P.M. daily, NZ$20. Evening city tour, 6:30 P.M. to 9 P.M. October to March, NZ$20. Full-day tours: Akaroa and cheese factory, 9 A.M. to 5 P.M., NZ$65, Hanmer Springs thermal resort 80 miles north), NZ$66. Pickup from hotels in metropolitan area.

H&H Travel Lines (The Gray Line), 40 Lichfield Street (799–120). City Roundabout Tour, 9:30 A.M. to 12:30 P.M., NZ$26. Blast from the Past Cruise on Lyttleton Harbour, including City Roundabout, 1:30 to 5 P.M. (except July), NZ$34. Tours depart Canterbury Information Center.

Pacific Tourways, 502A Wairakei Road (599–133). Garden City Tour, 9 A.M. to 11:30 A.M., 2 to 4:30 P.M. NZ$20. Full-day tour to Akaroa, 9 A.M. to 5:30 P.M., NZ$65. Four-day tour with 45-minute scenic flight and lunch on a high-country sheep station, 8 A.M. to 8 P.M., NZ$210. Full-day tour to Mount Cook and Queenstown, Tues. and Sat., departs 8 A.M.; NZ$420 including accommodations and breakfast.

Garden City Limousines (518–067). Private car rental at NZ$40 per hour for tours of the city, arts and crafts galleries, and thermal areas. *Garden City Cycle Tours* (799–395). 2-hour guided bike rides to scenic and historic sights, daily at 2 P.M., NZ$19.60. *Garden City Helicopters* (584–360). Tours take off daily, from NZ$35.

Dunedin. The two daily sightseeing tours by coach include: *Newton's Coachways'* city and suburbs tour (52–199), which leaves the Dunedin visitors center at 1:30 P.M. and covers either Larnach Castle, Olveston, and Glenfalloch or the Royal Albatross Colony and seals and penguins (in season). NZ$23.50.

Otago Harbour Cruises (774–215) offers 3½-hour nature cruises of Dunedin Harbour, departing at 2 and 3 P.M., NZ$20. *Southern Pride Tourism* (879–593) offers tours by horsedrawn carriage, three times each evening, NZ$4.40–NZ$11.

Franz Josef and Fox Glaciers. If you're not absolutely terrified of small aircraft and the weather is favorable you will miss an unforgettable experience if you don't take a scenic flight. The *Mount Cook Line* has 10 different flights by ski plane over the Franz Josef, Fox, Tasman, Meuller, and Hooker glaciers and over the main divide to Mount Cook. Some flights include a landing on the huge upper mountain snowfields by ski plane. At Franz Joseph phone 714; at Fox Glacier phone 812.

Glacier Helicopters, which holds a snow-landing-by-helicopter concession, operates flights over the Franz Josef, Fritz, Victoria, and Fox glaciers. Flights are from 10 to 30 minutes. At Franz Josef call 879.

Invercargill. City tours are run by *Panorama Tours* (82–419), starting at their terminal at the corner of Don and Kelvin sts. at 1:15 P.M., NZ$13.

Marlborough Sounds. Half- and full-day cruises are operated by *Friendship Cruises,* London Quay, Picton (phone 36–844). Fishing trips can be arranged, and small boats with outboards may be hired. For sailing in the sheltered waters of the Sound, 24-ft. motor sailers may be hired from *Southern Maritime Charters,* London Quay. Further information is available from the *Marlborough Public Relations Association,* Blenheim; phone (057) 84–480.

Milford Sound. See Queenstown, below.

Mount Cook. Tours of this mountain region can be arranged from Christchurch through *Guthrey's* (79–3560) and *Pacific Tourways* (599–133). For a ski plane flight, contact the *Mount Cook Line.*

Nelson. Personalized half- and full-day tours are conducted by *Nelson Day Tours* (76–674).

Queenstown. Sightseeing tours around Queenstown and to Arrowtown, including sites like the Cattledrome and the new kiwi and birdlife park, cost $13.50 for a half day and $31 for a full day. *H&H Group* has 9 A.M. and 2 P.M. tours to Skippers Canyon for $37.50. Skippers Canyon and Beyond is a 4½-hour tour including a chance to pan for gold. 8:30 A.M. and 1:30 P.M.; cost is NZ$43.

All major coach operators have day trips to Lake Manapouri for about NZ$110, including launch fare. Tours to the Routebourne and Greenstone Valleys cost $40 and NZ$46, respectively. Coaches leave Queenstown hotels at 7:15 A.M. and return at 8 P.M.

Bookings can be made through the *Mount Cook Travel Office* or the *NZTP Travel Office,* both downtown.

H&H Travel Lines runs a coach tour to the Routeburn and Greenstone valleys at the head of the lake. The tour departs at 9 A.M. and returns at 3 P.M. Nov. through May. Take your own lunch. Fares are NZ$40 to Routeburn and NZ$46 to Greenstone.

Milford Sound

Mount Cook Airlines will fly you over the spectacular scenery at Milford Sound, land you there for a brief exploration, or land you there for a 2-hour cruise down the Sound. Book at the Mount Cook office, Rees and Ballarat sts., or book *Milford Sound Scenic Flights* at any travel office or the airport.

Three coach lines operate daily return trips to Milford Sound. It is a long day, as the coaches leave Queenstown at 7:30 A.M. and return at 8 P.M., but the spectacular scenery makes it worthwhile. There's time for a launch cruise down Milford Sound. Book at the *Railways Road Services Office, H&H Travel Lines,* or the *NZTP Travel Office,* 49 Shotover St. (28–238).

The Remarkables

The newly developed ski field high in the Remarkables is in a previously inaccessible area. The road snakes up the edge of the mountain range to the base facilities at 4,500 ft., from which 6-seat gondolas take you up 15,000 ft. more. A short climb then takes you to Lookout Point, from which there are magnificent 180-degree panoramic views. The skiing area is clear of snow until about May, but its absence does not detract from the rugged beauty of the landscape. Mount Cook Line coaches have daily tours from 2:30 P.M., and the cost is NZ$22.

SPECIAL-INTEREST SIGHTSEEING. Dunedin. *Speight's Brewery* is one of the smallest breweries in New Zealand and is strictly regional, servicing Otago and Southland. But not long before the war its beer was shipped around the country, had won numerous international awards, and had an enviable reputation for quality. In northern ports its coastal ship became known as the Mercy Ship.

A rather unusual trip is a tour of the brewery at 200 Rattray St., just three blocks from the Octagon, at 10:30 A.M. Mon.–Fri. for NZ$2.20. Bookings are essential (779–480). The visitors center contains a collection of historic photographs and displays. On the tour visitors can see how barrels were made, see beer brewing in gleaming copper vessels, fermenting in open kauri vats, lagering in cold storage, being filtered and bottled in the packaging hall, and being loaded into the draught beer tankers—a feature of beer distribution in New Zealand. The tour is up to 2 hours long and, appropriately, concludes with a visit to the Board Room for a glass of Speight's Beer.

Queenstown. Visits to the *Walter Peak* sheep and cattle farms and *Mount Nicholas* sheep, cattle, deer, and horse farm make fascinating excursions. A half-day trip to either ranch by launch (the only means of access) is well worthwhile. Hosts explain how the steep hills are farmed and how sheep dogs are able to muster the animals from "the tops." Sheep-dog demonstrations are given. Walter Peak operates its own launch, which leaves the Queenstown launch jetty at 9:30 A.M. and 2 P.M., returning at 12:30 and 5 P.M. (reservations from any travel office), and the Cecil Peak launch leaves at 9:30 A.M. and 2:15 P.M., returning at noon and 4:45 P.M. Tickets are available from any travel office or the launch captains.

Aerial gondolas will take visitors 1,530 ft. above town to *Bob's Peak,* where a restaurant affords spectacular views. The terminal is at the corner of Isle and Brecon sts. The gondola operates 10 A.M.–5 P.M. and from 6:30 P.M. until the restaurant closes at midnight.

Earnslaw Cruises. It is hard to resist making a trip on this stately vintage steamer, which has plied the lake since 1912 and dominates the bay with its thin red funnel, its white hull, and its column of black smoke (just about the only pollution around Queenstown but excused because of the steamer's historic value). A 10 A.M. one-hour cruise (Aug. to June) is a restful break from other sightseeing (NZ$18). The one-hour evening cruise departs at 6 P.M. Fiordland Travel Services; phone 27–500.

Jet Boats. Several jet boats operate either from Queenstown Bay or the outlet of the Kawarau River and down the river *(Alpine Jet, Gold Stream Jet, Kawarau Jet, ProJet, Queenstown River Jet,* and *Twin Rivers Jet).* Durations range from 1 to 1½ hours and cost up to NZ$44. All depart hourly and courtesy transport from the Mount Cook Travel Office is provided if necessary (see Tours).

For added thrills, there are combinations of jet boats, helicopters, and rafts, such as *Helijet* (1½ hours, NZ$65), *ProJet/Helishuttle* (up to 2 hours, NZ$76), *ProJet/Raft* (3½ hours, NZ$76), *RiverJet/Helisights* (2 hours, NZ$76), *Triple Thriller* (3½ hours, NZ$99), and *Ultimate Three* (3½ hours, NZ$105). Check the tourist office for departure times.

Shotover Jet. Of all the jet-boat rides the *Shotover Jet* is the most spectacular and the most thrilling. It speeds along a stretch of the Shotover River which at first glance would appear to be unnavigable. Invented by a New Zealander, the boat has no propeller but is driven by a concentrated jet of water under high pressure, rather like a jet aircraft. They can travel in only 4 inches of water and maneuver quickly and easily through shallows and rapids, even turning in their own length.

Carrying up to nine passengers, the boat speeds through a narrow gorge, dodging boulders, over rapids and along shallow stretches only 1 foot in depth. Passengers wear life jackets, but this is purely a precautionary measure and there is no real danger. If the boat did happen to strike a boulder it would dent but not puncture. The trip starts below the Edith Cavell Bridge at Arthur's Point, about 3 miles from Queenstown, to which transport is provided at the Mount Cook Tourist Offices. Cost NZ$44.

Hydrofoil Cruise. A fully enclosed hydrofoil runs 20-minute cruises (NZ$15) at 11:30 A.M. and 1:15 P.M. and 50-minute scenic cruises (NZ$25) at 10:30 A.M., 2 P.M., and 3 P.M. from the jetty at the bottom of the mall.

Helicopter Flights. Helicopter flights vary from the Queenstown-sights trip to the more spectacular Grand Circle flights, which include a landing at almost the summit of the Remarkables. Fares range from NZ$33 for six minutes to NZ$132 for a tour of, and landing on, the Remarkables.

WILDLIFE. Christchurch. The *Willowbank Wildlife Reserve,* 60 Hussey Rd. (596–336), has the South Island's largest collection of birds and animals—including mountain lions, camels, Scottish highland cattle, primitive sheep, and other breeds of ancient livestock. Open daily, it's a 15-minute drive from city center.

Dunedin. To see the world's only mainland breeding spot for albatross, visit the *Royal Albatross Colony,* Taiaroa Heads, Otago Peninsula, 740–344 or 775–020. Accessible by tour, private car, or public transportation.

SPORTS. See also Facts at Your Fingertips, the introductory essay on fishing and hunting, and Mountain Climbing and Skiing below.

Queenstown

Hiking. The *Routeburn Walk* is a guided hike covering 25 miles and lasting 4 days. The trail is through Fiordland and Mt. Aspiring National Parks. Accommodations and meals provided. Contact Routeburn Walk, Ltd., Box 271, Queenstown (phone 28–200). The 4-day *Hollyford Valley Walk* also takes hikers through alpine scenery. Contact Fiordland National Park, Queenstown (phone 27–993).

Horseback riding. *Moonlight Stables* operates trail rides from Arthurs Point into an old gold-mining district. A coach carries visitors to and from the stables, beginning at the top of the mall on Camp St. Rates are $30 half day and $60 full day. Contact Moonlight Stables in Queenstown (phone 28–892).

Rafting. Whitewater rafting has become highly popular in both the North and South islands and especially at Queenstown. Contact the NZTP Travel Office.

Te Anau

Milford Track. Often called "the finest walk in the world," this five-day, 33-mile hike takes walkers from Te Anau to Milford Sound. Well-equipped huts provide overnight accommodations. Season is Nov. to April. Contact Tourist Hotel Corp., Box 2840, Wellington, or THC, Box 2207, Auckland, (09) 773–689.

MOUNTAIN CLIMBING. Contact *Mountain Guides, New Zealand,* Box 93, Twizel, (05) 620–737 or, for climbing in Mt. Cook National Park, *Alpine Guides,* Box 20, Mt. Cook National Park, (05) 621–834.

SKIING. *Mount Hutt,* two hours from Christchurch, offers varied terrain and 9 lifts, appropriate for all grades of skiers. Accommodations are also available less than an hour from the mountain in Ashburton. For more information contact Mt. Hutt International, Methven, Alpine Tourist Co., Box 446, Christchurch, (03) 792–720.

Mount Cook Ski Region. The highest peak in New Zealand offers a wide range of skiing adventures, including heliskiing, ski touring, and glacier skiing. Accommodations available. Write to the Ski Desk, THC Mt. Cook, Mt. Cook, New Zealand.

Highly popular are *Coronet Peak* and the *Remarkables* ski field at Queenstown. Contact the Mt. Cook Company.

Ideal for beginners is *Tekapo Ski Field.* A first-class ski school, rentals, and accommodations are available. Heli-skiing nearby. Contact Tekapo Ski Field, Box 7, Lake Tekapo, (05) 056–852.

For skiing, including helisking and glacier skiing trips, contact *Alpine Guides,* Box 20, Mt. Cook, (05) 621–834; *Live-Life New Zealand, Ltd.,* Box 4517, Auckland, (09) 768–936; *Mountain Guides New Zealand,* Box 93, Twizel, (05) 630–737.

MUSEUMS AND HISTORIC SITES. Christchurch. *The Arts Center of Christchurch,* in an old neo-Gothic building on Worcester St. (60–989), Monday–Friday 8:30 A.M.–5 P.M. A living center including theater, ballet, cinema, craft workshop, potters, cane and stained-glass workers and printmakers.

Brooke Gifford Gallery, 112 Manchester St. (65–288), Mon.–Fri. 10:30 A.M.–5 P.M. Exhibitions of contemporary New Zealand painting and sculpture.

Canterbury Museum, on Rolleston Ave. (68–379), houses a good, permanent Antarctica exhibit, along with displays of New Zealand's history, natural life, and Maori culture. Open Mon.–Sat., 10 A.M.–4:30 P.M.; opens 2 P.M. Sun. Admission is free; donations encouraged. Just behind the museum is the *McDougall Art Gallery*

(50–915) housing exhibits of Australasian and European Art. 10 A.M.–4:30 P.M. Mon.–Fri.; 1–5:30 P.M. weekends.

Canterbury Society of Arts, 66 Gloucester St., 67–261, Mon.–Fri. 10 A.M.–4:30 P.M. Displays of New Zealand and overseas art.

Ferrymead Historic Park is a working museum of transport and technology situated on 100 acres at 269 Bridle Path Rd., Heathcote, near the Cashmere Hills. Exhibits include vintage machinery, automobiles, horse carts, trolley cars, railroad locomotives, aircraft, home appliances, musical instruments, and models. A ride in a vintage train or trolley is the way to reach a vintage township with an operating bakery and printing works. It is open daily from 10 A.M. to 4:30 P.M. and can be reached by bus from Cathedral Square. For more information call 841–708.

Dunedin. The *Otago Early Settlers' Museum,* at 220 Cumberland St. (close to the Railway Station; call 775–052), shows early colonial household items in authentic settings, including 19th-century toys and costumes and early pianos and printing equipment. Open 9 A.M.–4:30 P.M. weekdays; 10:30 A.M.–4:30 P.M. Sat; Oct.–March; from 1:30 P.M. Sun. Small admission charge.

The *Otago Museum* on Great King St. (three blocks from the Octagon; call 772–372, contains a good collection of Polynesian and Melanesian exhibits, ceramics and New Zealand birds. 10 A.M.–5 P.M. Mon.–Fri.

The *Dunedin Public Art Gallery* in Logan Park (a short taxi ride) is the oldest art gallery in New Zealand and has a good coverage of New Zealand and foreign paintings. Open 10 A.M.–4:40 P.M., Mon.–Fri., 2–5 P.M. weekends and holidays.

Out on the Otago Peninsula, 9 miles beyond Dunedin on Highcliff Rd., stands *Larnach Castle,* where the declaration was signed giving women the right to vote (1893: a precedent in the western world). The castle was built by William Larnach for his first wife. The restored interior is elaborately decorated with architectural touches from all periods. The carved dining room ceiling took some 14 years to complete. (Larnach shot himself when his third wife ran away with his son.) Newton's Sightseeing Bus includes the castle on a tour—or you can take your own car. Accommodations and dining available. Open 9 A.M.–5 P.M. in winter; until dusk at other seasons. Phone 761–302.

Olveston was another unique home, built around 1905. One mile from Dunedin, on Cobden St., off Queens Dr. (773–320), it reflects the elegant lifestyle of the businessman who built it. The building, a Jacobean work of art in itself, houses art treasures from around the world. Reservations recommended for guided tours. Newton's Sightseeing Tours also include this.

Queenstown. *Arrowtown* is 14 miles northeast of Queenstown—and a trip into the past. Once filled with gold miners from all over the world, the town remains one of the prettiest in New Zealand. There are the Lake District Centennial Museum, a pub that once served the miners, an old stone jail, and a variety of shops. H & H coaches depart from the Camp St. depot at 2 P.M.

The *Queenstown Motor Museum,* 25 Brecon St. (phone 752), is a 5-minute walk from the center of town. The display here is of vintage, veteran, and classic vehicles. Open daily; small admission charge.

ARTS. See Museums and Historic Sites, above.

INDEX

Index

Fodor's Travel Guides

U.S. Guides

Alaska
American Cities
The American South
Arizona
Atlantic City & the
  New Jersey Shore
Boston
California
Cape Cod
Carolinas & the
  Georgia Coast
Chesapeake
Chicago
Colorado
Dallas & Fort Worth
Disney World & the
  Orlando Area

The Far West
Florida
Greater Miami,
  Fort Lauderdale,
  Palm Beach
Hawaii
Hawaii (Great Travel
  Values)
Houston & Galveston
I-10: California to
  Florida
I-55: Chicago to New
  Orleans
I-75: Michigan to
  Florida
I-80: San Francisco to
  New York

I-95: Maine to Miami
Las Vegas
Los Angeles, Orange
  County, Palm Springs
Maui
New England
New Mexico
New Orleans
New Orleans (Pocket
  Guide)
New York City
New York City (Pocket
  Guide)
New York State
Pacific North Coast
Philadelphia
Puerto Rico (Fun in)

Rockies
San Diego
San Francisco
San Francisco (Pocket
  Guide)
Texas
United States of
  America
Virgin Islands
  (U.S. & British)
Virginia
Waikiki
Washington, DC
Williamsburg,
  Jamestown &
  Yorktown

Foreign Guides

Acapulco
Amsterdam
Australia, New Zealand
  & the South Pacific
Austria
The Bahamas
The Bahamas (Pocket
  Guide)
Barbados (Fun in)
Beijing, Guangzhou &
  Shanghai
Belgium & Luxembourg
Bermuda
Brazil
Britain (Great Travel
  Values)
Canada
Canada (Great Travel
  Values)
Canada's Maritime
  Provinces
Cancún, Cozumel,
  Mérida, The
  Yucatán
Caribbean
Caribbean (Great
  Travel Values)

Central America
Copenhagen,
  Stockholm, Oslo,
  Helsinki, Reykjavik
Eastern Europe
Egypt
Europe
Europe (Budget)
Florence & Venice
France
France (Great Travel
  Values)
Germany
Germany (Great Travel
  Values)
Great Britain
Greece
Holland
Hong Kong & Macau
Hungary
India
Ireland
Israel
Italy
Italy (Great Travel
  Values)
Jamaica (Fun in)

Japan
Japan (Great Travel
  Values)
Jordan & the Holy Land
Kenya
Korea
Lisbon
Loire Valley
London
London (Pocket Guide)
London (Great Travel
  Values)
Madrid
Mexico
Mexico (Great Travel
  Values)
Mexico City & Acapulco
Mexico's Baja & Puerto
  Vallarta, Mazatlán,
  Manzanillo, Copper
  Canyon
Montreal
Munich
New Zealand
North Africa
Paris
Paris (Pocket Guide)

People's Republic of
  China
Portugal
Province of Quebec
Rio de Janeiro
The Riviera (Fun on)
Rome
St. Martin/St. Maarten
Scandinavia
Scotland
Singapore
South America
South Pacific
Southeast Asia
Soviet Union
Spain
Spain (Great Travel
  Values)
Sweden
Switzerland
Sydney
Tokyo
Toronto
Turkey
Vienna
Yugoslavia

Special-Interest Guides

Bed & Breakfast
  Guide: North America
  1936...On the
  Continent

Royalty Watching
Selected Hotels of
  Europe

Selected Resorts
  and Hotels of the U.S.
Ski Resorts of North
  America

Views to Dine by
  around the World